SUN, SAND AND CEMENT

ROSTERS LTD

SUN, SAND AND CEMENT

Cheryl Taylor

ROSTERS LTD

Published by Rosters Ltd
23 Welbeck St, London, W1

First edition 1986
Reprinted 1988
Second edition 1991
© Cheryl Taylor

ISBN: 0-948032-89-8

Printed and bound in Great Britain by
Cox & Wyman Ltd, Reading

PREFACE

This is the second edition of our popular guide to buying a home overseas. The first guide was published in 1986 and concentrated largely on Continental Europe. It was a time when the UK housing market and stock market were both booming. Buying a second home overseas, particularly in Spain, became very popular. As we enter the nineteen nineties the situation has changed. High interest rates at home and a downturn in the economy mean that it is even more vital to choose a home abroad that represents sound value for money. With the advent of 1992 and the promise of lower air fares within the EEC a holiday home on the continent should become more affordable. However, we have widened the coverage considerably in the second edition to include Exotic Islands and Far Away Places where we feel real value is available. We welcome correspondence from readers who wish to pass on tips or warnings we can consider for subsequent editions.

Rosemary Burr, Editor.

ABOUT THE AUTHOR

Cheryl Taylor is an experienced freelance journalist who specialises in writing international property pieces and articles on financial matters. Her work has appeared in many specialist magazines as well as the national press. She wrote the first edition of this guide in 1986 and since then has closely watched developments in key areas such as timeshare, the development of the French property market for overseas buyers and the new methods of funding overseas property. In updating this book she has drawn on her extensive travels worldwide and the experience of many people who have already joined the foreign property set.

Introduction:
A PLACE IN THE SUN

Twenty years ago an overseas home was a rich man's privilege. Now thousands of British people are buying a little piece of sunshine. Their motives are mixed. Some simply want to beat those spiralling holiday costs. Others hope to profit by renovating a crumbling rural retreat. Many more are just seeking a retirement home.

Freedom from exchange controls means that there are no longer expensive and prohibitive restrictions on buying property abroad. Quite literally the world is your oyster. With so much choice, picking the right spot for your home can be a daunting task. There are plenty of pitfalls lurking to trap the unwary. Complex tax and legal rules, botched construction and unscrupulous property developers, to name but a few.

This book will help guide you safely through this minefield stage by stage. Whether your dream home in the sun is a tiny apartment on the Costa del Sol or luxurious villa on the French Riviera, it will help smooth the path to your new front door.

CONTENTS

Chapter One:
BEFORE YOU SPLASH OUT

Before you decide to buy a villa or flat overseas you'll need to ask yourself some crucial questions. That way you'll have a more realistic idea of the type of property you should be considering.

Sorting out the options

1. How much money are you prepared to spend?
You have to take into account the initial cost of the property, its upkeep and the cost of living in the country of your choice. Don't forget the old bogey of inflation, which is still an important factor in many countries overseas. Another factor is the likely cost of travelling to your home in the sun, especially if you plan to use it for regular holidays.

2. What sort of accommodation do you need?
Basically, the key point to decide is whether you are simply looking for a holiday home or a suitable residence for long stays and possibly retirement. Obviously this will affect both the size of the accommodation you will need, the facilities and sometimes the location.

3. Where do you feel most 'at home'?
It's important to see even your favourite haunt in all its difference guises. The changing seasons often bring a shift of perspective. That idyllic holiday resort in August can turn into a ghost town in November. A short three month season will be

bad for letting and could turn your dream spot into a depressing nightmare as a retirement location.

4. What kind of lifestyle do you enjoy?
A carefree ethnic existence may be cheap and cheerful but a craving for fish fingers and baked beans washed down with a pint of best bitter could prove expensive on the Rivieria.

5. What are your priorities?
Make a list of features that are essential, followed by those things you would like to be included at the resort or location of your ultimate choice. You may be seeking sunshine, beaches and good food. Alternatively, you may prefer mountains, ski slopes and good communications.

6. What standard of facilities do you want?
Roughly speaking the more facilities you need, the higher the price. If you want seclusion it's unlikely that you can expect a prompt service from the electricity man if the fuses blow. If you are planning to retire, check that medical facilities are adequate and you can afford to pay the bills.

7. Do you want an old or new property?
Old properties may be cheaper and have more character but they can also lead to more problems when it comes to basics such as wiring and plumbing, not to say hassles of restoration. People tend to underestimate the work involved in making an old home liveable. Ask yourself whether you want to devote valuable holiday time to decorating and building.

8. How much travelling are you prepared to do?
Work out exactly how long it will take door-to-door from your present home.

9. Which seasons of the year and for how many weeks each year, are you, your family and friends going to use the house or flat?
The home you are considering may be marvellous fun during the summer, but dead as a do-do for nine months of the year.

10. Do you want to let the property when it's not being used by you or your family?

This sounds a marvellous idea in theory. In practice, many people prefer to keep the property for their own personal use, leaving their treasured belongings and furniture untouched by hordes of visitors. Apart from sentimental considerations, letting is easier said than done. There's tax, insurance and a whole host of other costs to consider.

Key Questions

To avoid being dubbed an 'innocent abroad' and landing yourself into a financial mess, you should line up a series of pertinent questions to fire at the prospective agent or developer.

a) Is the property being offered with clear title, free of encumbrance?

In plain English does the property belong to the chap trying to flog it. Often, it is quite common for properties to be jointly owned by several members of a family and it may not be sold without the consent of all concerned. Another common problem which frequently arises is that developers take out mortgages to finance the construction and may not be in a position to conclude the sale. You should ask your solicitor to check these points for you.

b) Are there any additional costs which you will incur to provide basic services such as water, electricity, drainage or telephones?

If these facilities have not been installed, you should make full provision for the extra bills you are likely to run up. In remote areas this can be quite hefty.

c) What additional costs will be involved in the purchase?

The total cost will take account of solicitor's fees, conveyancing charges, tax, surveys and possibly a couple of flying visits to the site.

d) Are there any local regulations which affect the purchase of property by foreigners?
Some countries extend a less warm welcome to foreign buyers than others. Nearly all impose a series of formalities. Make sure you comply with these from the start.

e) Will you find it easy to sell the property?
There's a whole host of factors to consider here, including any restrictions of bringing money home and the size of the market for homes of the quality you are examining. Plus, your own tax position and likely tax bill.

f) Could the property's value be hard hit by further developments?
Check whether there are any plans for future construction in the area and what scope is available to developers in the vicinity.

g) What are the annual running costs likely to be?
You should take into account the fact that you'll be away for a large part of the year and you may not wish to leave the property unattended. Try and find out the cost of hiring a local company to maintain the property during your absence.

h) How much will you need to spend on furniture, repairs, alterations?
A difficult question. Check whether any furniture is included in the price. If so, is its quality sufficiently high. Also, consider any costs involved with the garden or surrounding land, if appropriate. Plus, many countries unfortunately share the same sort of security problems as we have in some of our inner cities, so you may need to spend some money on making your home safe.

i) What are the realistic possibilities of earning an income from letting the property?
Check whether there are any restrictions on letting, a letting service, the estimated level of return and whether any income from this source will be taxable overseas.

4

j) How much will it cost to travel to your home in the sun?
Try and find out whether there are any special low cost flights and reduced rate car hire facilities.

A reputable estate agent or developer should have no difficulty in providing detailed answers to these questions. However, don't forget it is their job to sell you a property. The estate agent will earn commission on the sale and the developer obviously has a direct financial interest.

Do's and Don'ts

DON'T buy sight unseen. Buying a holiday on the basis of pretty pictures in a brochure is one thing, but buying a holiday home in the same way is not to be recommended. You wouldn't buy a property at home without giving it the once-over, so don't alter your standards when considering a purchase abroad.

DO buy through a recognised estate agent, preferably one specialising in the country of your choice.

DO take proper legal advice. Ideally you should use two solicitors, your own and one with a good track record in the country you are planning to invest. Never sign anything in a foreign language without first having a translation and agreeing this with the other party to the deal.

DON'T take anyone at face value. A little extra checking at this early stage is invaluable. Check the financial credibility of the agent or developer you are dealing with plus full particulars about the property and legal situation in the country of your choice.

DON'T make a snap decision at the end of an inspection trip. Most reputable companies provide inexpensive inspection trips, where you can often stay in the type of villa or apartment which you intend to buy. If the development is selling fast, you may be asked for a small deposit. Check

5

whether this is returnable. Don't part with more than say £100 to £200. Speak to your solicitor first.

DO make full use of the inspection trip. Have a good look around, try to talk to existing owners and be fully armed with a list of relevant questions.

DON'T sign anything or part with any money without checking first with your solicitor. A good rule of thumb, which will give you a breathing space to consider the transaction in the cold light of a British morning and help you avoid rash commitments you'll find difficult to finance.

DON'T buy when you are on holiday. That warm glow quickly fades and if you still feel enthusiastic later on there's nothing to stop you going back to choose a suitable property.

DO try to assess the all-year-round potential of your holiday or retirement home. Some places vibrate in the summer but then take on a forlorn and deserted air in winter. That's bad news if you intend to let during the winter months and could be depressing if you plan to retire there.

DON'T buy without checking out the local area in some depth. Try to draw up a dossier on the locality. If possible talk to existing British owners and discover what sort of problems they have met. Check out local amenities, tax, shopping, furniture, building costs and wages. Also take into account general economic conditions such as inflation and potential exchange controls.

DO check to see if the developer has a guarantee of completion from a bank or insurance company. This is the best protection you as a buyer can have. Your solicitor can do this for you. Remember you can't obtain title to an apartment until the entire building is complete.

6

DON'T pay up-front for an uncompleted flat or villa. Insist on stage payments and make sure these are geared to genuine progress. Get your solicitor to check there is sufficient security for these instalments should the developer become insolvent.

DO check your property is not being built on greenbelt, military land or an unsuitable piece of land. The local land registry is the best source of information on these matters and your solicitor should investigate before you sign any documents.

DON'T leave any phrase in the contract unexplained. A seemingly innocuous clause such as 'subject to local conditions' can spell doom if you are on a fixed price contract.

DO consider the condition of the property you hope to buy. Arrange for an independent survey and compare costs locally. The Institute of Chartered Surveyors, based in London, are well qualified to advise on this.

DON'T expect a cash bonanza from letting. Regular letting may produce a gross annual return of up to 12% – but that's before tax. Some property companies offer letting contracts with an annual income ranging from 5% to 12% depending on the size and location of your home. However, you may well be restricted in the times you can use the property for your own use. Watch out for the small print. The company may deduct running costs and maintenance from your gross income.

DO think ahead. Many properties are dream homes for three years and are on the market again after five years. Try to minimise risks by sticking to countries with political stability and without a history of restricting flow of money in and out.

Chapter Two:
FRANCE NOUVEAU

If you are looking for creature comforts rather than romantic rural retreats, France offers a range of up-to-date accommodation with all mod. cons. Although, it pays to remember that most new flats will have smaller rooms, and even the best French plumbing sometimes leaves a little to be desired. Modern apartments range from tiny studios (not much bigger than an average broom-cupboard), to five roomed luxury penthouses. The French count the number of rooms, not bedrooms and prices rise the higher up in the block the flat is situated.

Although stamp duty will be lower on property built within the last five years, VAT of 18.6 per cent is payable on newly-built homes. This is usually included in the quoted price, but do check. To cater for the modern tourist many developers, including some from Britain, have built multi-purpose complexes consisting of a variety of different types of accommodation, plus a range of sporting facilities.

The French Riviera
The British made the French Riviera fashionable over 100 years ago, and it has kept its snob appeal. The Mediterranean coast, sometimes referred to as the Côte d'Azur, which stretches from Menton to St. Tropez, remains the magnet for those Brits in search of sun, sea and sophistication. Prices are far from cheap, but properties here hold their values well and are always in demand. A studio apartment in Cannes starts at £60,000 for a flat ordinaire. Middle range holiday apartments,

usually built in complexes with swimming pools and tennis courts, start at £150,000 for two bedrooms. A top notch flat could set you back £250,000. The exact price will reflect location, facilities and proximity to the beach.

One of the most expensive spots is still the fashionable St. Tropez. A diminutive studio starts at about £80,000. A villa is likely to retail at between £400,000 and £500,000 in one of the celebrity studded neighbourhoods. Those prepared to rub shoulders with the less famous will need at least £150,000 for a small house. There are a number of resorts and villages along the coast, many with marinas, which are particularly popular with yachtsmen. These vary considerably in price and quality.

Port Grimaud is one of the prettiest, and the most expensive. A waterfront city, with a maze of canals, bridges, islands and promontories. These are cafes, squares, restaurants and even a church. It all looks like one of the older and nicer bits of the south of France, but in fact it's practically brand new. The project began in 1969 and is now complete. Resales occasionally appear on the market, priced from £80,000 for a studio, £150,000 for a tiny cottage and from £250,000 for a three bedroom house.

Although the coast is highly developed, a short drive into the hills delivers you into the natural seclusion of some lovely countryside with a sprinkling of medieval hilltop villages. Prices slip as you travel inland. In the historic hilltop village of Grimaud several new apartment blocks have been built, with pale Provençal colour-washed walls, and not a new brick in sight to betray their youth. Prices range from £40,000 for a studio, rising to £150,000 for a three bedroom flat, overlooking the Bay of St. Tropez.

New homes at Domaine des Mas de St. Pierre, on the edge of the village of Plan de la Tour in the foothills of the Massif des Maures, near Ste. Maxime, are simple and rustic. However, they all have modern kitchens and baths, and prices are reasonable. One bedroom terraced houses start at £50,000, two bedrooms from £68,000 and from £92,000 for three. Leisure facilities include a swimming pool and tennis courts.

Agents: Domus Abroad, 4, Gardnor Road, London NW3, handle a selection of newly-built and resale properties in the South of France.

Ski resorts

These are a popular choice as most resorts cater for both winter and summer visitors. Again, prices vary depending upon location, but you should expect to pay from £36,000 for a small studio, £67,000 for two bedrooms, and £100,000 for a chalet styled duplex sleeping six. International high altitude resorts are traditionally great favourites with the Brits. These include Val d'Isere, Meribel, La Plagne and Avoriaz. Prices fetch as much as £100,000 for one bedroom in the fashionable resorts of Val d'Isere. But this resort is considered by 'afficionados' to offer the best skiing in the world.

Steady favourites are the hamlets of Valmorel and Belle Plagne, within the La Plagne domaine. Valmorel is a new resort set at 1,400 metres in the heart of Savoie. It typifies the type of accommodation available in newer resorts. Construction follows traditional chalet style, the village centre is traffic free and the chalets are grouped together in hamlets. Sporting facilities are good and there is a kindergarten.

The skiing is suitable for everyone from beginners to experts. There are 150kms of pistes, forty-five lifts and eighty different runs. Prices start at £36,000 for a furnished studio, rising to £100,000 for a three-bedroom apartment. Most flats have good views and come equipped with fitted kitchens, modern bathrooms and balconies.

For ski buffs who want to play in the snow all year round the new resort of Belle Plagne, 2,050 metres up, is worth considering. The accommodation is based on log cabins. Skiing starts at the enormous snowfield of the Bellecote glacier. The 15km run drops progressively over 2,050 metres along one of the longest runs in the Alps.

There are also a number of traditional Alpine villages, at lower altitudes, of which the most attractive are St. Martin Belleville and Les Coches. Situated in the three Valleys, both locations have access to the high skiing to the Val Thorens,

Meribel and Courcheval. Apartments in the old Alpine village of St. Martin de Belleville start at £48,000 for one bedroom.

Les Coches, perched on a forest hillside within the La Plagne network, is very pretty and provides a good location for families. Leaseback is a popular deal here. For a reduced price, say £28,000 for a flat worth £38,000, you can use the flat for up to six weeks each year in return for surrendering the rental rights for 11 years.

A French Company, Pierre et Vacances, are selling flats in prime South of France and skiing locations at lease-back prices ranging from £28,000 for a studio at Les Coches, to £50,000 for a three-bedroom flat in Cannes. One of the benefits of this sort of deal is that there are no charges to pay for 11 years – no management fees, taxes or maintenance costs. You also own the title, which you wouldn't under the timeshare system.

Agents: Frank Rutherford & Co.

Chapter Three:
FRANCE ANCIEN

The Channel Tunnel is planned to open in the 1990s and for the past two years the Brits have been flocking to France to cash in on the predicted property boom. Prices are rising rapidly as more buyers discover that parts of Normandy and Brittany are considerably cheaper than southern England. However, those who dabble in the French residential property market will quickly discover there are few fat profits to be made. The tumble-down cottage or farmhouse 'ripe for renovation', is likely to be offered at a price which is unreasonable by French standards; even if it is cheap compared with prices at home. Restoration costs are high, and the French taxman will swallow a large proportion of any profit made on resale.

Undeterred by rising costs and taxes, the British invasion continues at the rate of 50,000 French properties a year. Even British farmers are getting in on the act, attracted by the lure of cheap French agricultural land at prices half those on the other side of the Channel. There has been a slowing of the market in northern France, much hyped in recent years, occasioned by high-interest rates in Britain and uncertainty about the future of the Chunnel. Despite this English invasion the French housing market does not demonstrate as much fluctuation as we are used to in Britain. If it were not for the interest of 'Les Anglais', house prices in the north would be static, if not falling. Indeed, there is still a danger that many English might buy property they can only sell to other English buyers.

Away from the English-invaded north, property prices are more realistic. Prices vary according to area, the location of the

12

property and its condition. Anything fashionable or 'bourgeois' is expensive, and possibly 'listed'. The French control listed buildings, inside and out, which effectively bans alterations. Prices also depend on the quality of the land on which it stands. Poor quality agricultural land will go for about £300 an acre; richer soil £1,000 an acre.

Châteaux

The days of snapping up 'une petite maison à la campagne', ripe for renovation and going for a song, are almost gone. However, France is bristling with cheap, cast-off châteaux for sale because the young French are fleeing the countryside, and the old aristocratic families whose fortunes are diluted by the law obliging Frenchmen to bequeath their property equally to all their offspring are often deeply in hock to the bank for essential repairs and feeling the pinch. The majority sell for below £250,000, due to the current wealth tax imposed on the value of an estate. You can still buy a run-down château, with a dozen rooms, complete with a moat and a few acres of parkland, for as little as £90,000. But, to get a habitable home a sum of at least £150,000 would be required.

There are thousands of 'grands châteaux' in France, many of them in a state of decay – like fairy-tale giants gracefully crumbling into their moats; irresistibly charming, but damp, draughty and a constant drain on the bank balance. It takes a certain kind of person to take on one of these grand old dragons. Medieval stone walls, flagged floors and ballroom-sized bedrooms are hardly cosy, and grand staircases and vaulted ceilings cost a fortune to heat. One château owner who had installed central heating estimated that his winter heating bill topped £2,000.

A château can be a large country house or a fortified castle, so vast it could house an army of guests. The majority are to be found in northern France, particularly in the Loire. The genuine ones are those which are the right style for the area they were built; the most valuable are those built before the end of the seventeenth century. A 'gentilhommiere' – an eighteenth century nobleman's house, with about six bedrooms and four reception rooms, is a more manageable proposition. Listed châteaux will qualify for grants for repair and maintenance, especially when the owner is prepared to allow public access.

Renovating a rustic retreat

If you have the necessary skills there's both fun and value to be had in renovating a farmhouse, cottage or barn. One of the big pluses about buying this type of property is that they usually come with at least half an acre of land, maybe more.

So what can you expect? Generally, three or four rooms are just about habitable. Usually you'll need to add cooking and hot water facilities, possibly by building a kitchen. You may also have to put in bathroom and toilet facilities. The flooring may also need attention. Concrete or wood should be laid over earthen floors. Heating is another prime consideration. Winter evenings in many parts of France have a decided chilly air which is easy to forget in the warm after glow of a mid-summer day.

Do make sure the roof is sound. Repairs here can prove costly. As a rough yardstick you should set aside a sum equivalent to the cost of the property for essential repairs. Don't fall in love with a rural retreat which lacks mains water and electricity. If you do, your dream home could well turn into a financial nightmare. Other costs to take into account are the agent's commission, 4 per cent if a French agent is used as in France the buyer pays, and various legal fees. All in all, this usually adds up to 10 per cent of the purchase price. British agents selling French properties include the commission in the asking price.

Those in search of wrecks and ruins to restore should head for Normandy, Brittany, Burgundy, Languedoc/Roussillon, the Dordogne and the Charante. There you will find the cream of the 'wrecks' at the best prices. A number of British agents such as Frank Rutherford, Property Consultants and French & Associates, specialise in handling properties in these areas.

14

Normandy and Brittany

Conveniently placed for a quick hop to France, the Pas de Calais is the area that has attracted the most interest. Because of its favourable situation, particularly for the British weekender, old country properties are quickly snapped up. Prices have doubled in the past two years, and there is little left for under £30,000. You could buy a dilapidated two-roomed cottage close to Calais for £32,000 or a derelict seventeenth century farmhouse for £40,000.

Further inland the scenery improves and property prices become more reasonable. The great advantages of Normandy and Brittany are accessibility and the rugged beauty of the landscape. Some distance from Paris, which means prices are lower and the area has retained much of its rural charm.

Summer temperatures are warmer and drier than in Southern England, the food is wonderful and the beaches the best in northern Europe. Both regions are tailor-made for traditional rustic retreats, with prices to suit most pockets. Newly-built homes are thin on the ground and consequently pricier.

Normandy has the cream of the farmhouses and châteaux, while Brittany offers better value in rural stone cottages and agricultural dwellings. Traditional thatched cottages, converted 'pressoirs' − cider houses, and old black and white timbered farmhouses are popular with British buyers.

Prices range from about £20,000 for a ramshackle two-roomed cottage in deepest Brittany. However, you would need to spend at least another £20,000 to make it habitable. An unconverted sixteenth century farmhouse in Normandy, with stables, outbuildings, and a few acres of land would cost closer to £60,000. A more basic farmbuilding, with a rambling old barn and a well, begins at about £30,000, and a pristine Normandy mansion, timbered black and white, with six bed-rooms, and all mod cons costs closer to £90,000.

Local agent Henri Gravans, based in Falaise, Normandy, (40/ 42, Rue Trinité, BP 64, 14700 Falise, Tel. 31 40 12 12) has several such properties on his books.

Several UK agents handle property for sale in France. French

Property Consultants Frank Rutherford & Co. (7, Chelsea Manor Street, London SW3 Tel. 071-351 4454) has been active in France for almost 20 years. It offers a range of properties throughout the country, from ruins to the fully renovated. Rutherford's offerings range from about £15,000 for the ruined shell of a Brittany cottage, to about £125,000 for an eighteenth century 'gentilhommiere', fully restored, with six bedrooms and many original features, set in almost three hectares of park and woodland.

A simple village house, two hundred years old and scarcely modernised, will set you back from around £18,000. The converted version, with beamed ceilings, original stone fire-places, and modern kitchen and bath, will cost anything from £40,000. A traditional Breton granite cottage with steeply sloping roof, thick walls, a Dutch barn and a couple of acres of agricultural land, starts at £35,000.

Coastal prices start at about £20,000, but expect to pay £25,000 plus for anything habitable. The Cherbourg peninsula, right down to Mont St. Michel is cheap and good value. A five-roomed farmhouse in need of some modernisation would cost £25,000. The whole area is great for yachtsmen – or for letting to the yachting fraternity.

Loire

Prices in the Loire are low and unlikely to rise because of its cool damp climate. It was once the most aristocratic part of France, even if most of its gilded châteaux are owned by rock stars and rubber millionaires these days. Châteaux are thick on the ground in varying stages of dilapidation. For about £150,000, you can buy a turreted château, with eight bedrooms and five reception rooms, surrounded by 10 acres of parkland. A château can cost from £100,000 to £400,000, though most would swallow another £100,000 spent on repairs and redecoration.

Recent offerings in the Loire on Rutherford's books include the fifteenth century Château de Laveau, situated between Samur and Angers. The property includes 30 acres of wooded parkland and a double moat, plus pavillion, farmbuildings and grande salle. Its owner is asking £290,000 for the nine bedroom, nine bathroom house which has been largely restored, but would need another £50,000 spent on rewiring and installing a proper heating system. The Loire has plenty of more modestly priced gems; ranging in price between £15,000 for a small village house to £50,000 for a converted farmhouse, with a barn as big as a detached house.

The Dordogne, Charante and Charante Maritime
The area based around Périgeux, the capital of the Dordogne, is dotted with truffle farms, forts, and fairy-tale castles. To go with this, it has wonderful scenery, excellent food and some very good wines. These days, trying to find inexpensive older properties to restore in the Dordogne is like looking for a needle in a haystack. With about 6,000 Brits already in place, the supply of unconverted village houses and farmhouses has virtually dried up. There is little left for under £50,000 and prices continue to rise.

The Charante, with its soft rolling countryside unscarred by motorways and tourist hordes, offers more. It has a strong supply of stone-cottages and is an hour nearer to the Channel Ports. Prices are half those in the Dordogne; £35,000 is the top price, and there are plenty around for under £15,000.

This is the Cognac area of France and is south of the Loire, the great divide in climatic terms. The weather is warmer, houses are bigger, and you can still get an old village house to convert for £8,000. A four-roomed stone farmhouse, requiring renovation, with about half an acre costs around £20,000.

Old properties in the Charante represent some of the best value available at the time of writing. When weighing up the asking price make sure you check out the adjacent barns and outbuildings. There is often three times as much space in the barnyard as the cottage itself. Most houses have thick limestone walls, often lurking under plaster, which are particularly attractive when exposed. An added bonus is that most properties are linked into the main supply of water and electricity.

Rock bottom in the price chart would be four walls of a barn for the princely sum of £2,000. There's a snag, you might have to negotiate vacant possession with a pig and a couple of geese. An old barn overgrown with apple trees would cost £5,000 and need a further £10,000 to make it barely habitable. A dilapidated village house, set in an enclosed courtyard with hollyhocks round the door, with an attached barn that would convert to a self contained house, costs about £8,000. Old farmhouses are thick on the ground, in conditions ranging from simply derelict to a pile of stones. With oak beamed ceilings and flagstone floors, untouched by modern conveniences, these cost in the region of £20,000.

Roussillon – Languedoc
The area around Perpignan is the poor man's Riviera with its Mediterranean coast and its rugged hinterland scattered with pretty hilltop villages. Hot and dry in summer, property prices are much cheaper than on the Côte D'Azur. Village houses, usually clustered around a square, a church and a boules pitch, cost from £30,000 unrestored.

Provence
Property in Provence is pricey; £90,000 will buy you an unconverted Provençal 'mas' – a chic farmhouse, and half an acre. However, it may be at least a two hours' drive from the sea. Such properties suitable for restoration are sought-after and becoming harder to find, therefore expensive.

Much of the hinterland in the warm fashionable south has already been scoured by bargain hunters, and to find unrestored rusticity you will need to travel to the 'département' of The Var. This corner of Provence, inland from Cannes, has a number of rural properties, the possibilities of which have yet to be fully realised. An old farmhouse requiring renovation, with three acres of land might be found for around £48,000 in the Lac du Verdon area. Traditionally, the farmer lived upstairs, and kept his animals on the ground floor. This cattle-store could be converted to double the living area of the house.

Some of the lowest prices are to be found around the ancient market town of Aups, with its narrow, winding streets and tall shuttered houses. A London estate agency, Domus Abroad, run by Francophile Maurice Lazarus (4, Gardnor Road, Hampstead, London NW3 Tel 071-409 0571) has teamed up with a local agent, offering a choice of part-renovated properties. Studios in a restored stone-walled Aups building, can be bought for as little as £14,000. A two-bedroom attic flat, approached by steep stairs, with a tiny roof terrace, from £27,000. A big plus is that you are only an hour or so from St. Tropez.

Chapter Four:
ITALY

Lakes, mountains, history and culture provide the tourist bait in a country that has continued to enchant since the days of the Grand Tour of Europe. Culture vultures, sun seekers and those simply looking for a change of pace can all find something to satisfy them in Italy.

It is a country of beauty, contrasts and perhaps most of all, a living museum of ancient civilisation and renaissance art. Sightseeing is a major occupation and those of sporty nature can enjoy some of the best skiing resorts in Europe and some of the finest beaches along the Venetian Riviera.

The Italians are friendly and gregarious. Many speak English but if you are considering living there a good smattering of Italian is worth its weight in gold.

Prices are not cheap. The cost of living in Rome, Milan, Naples and Florence is high and the fashionable Riviera, so popular with the natives, is very expensive.

The market for properties geared exclusively towards foreigners is relatively small. A handful of new developments exist in Tuscany, Umbria and the Italian Lakes but you need to be prepared for some tramping around the countryside to discover your dream property.

Tuscany
The Italian economy is on its way up, and this is reflected in the local property market. Values have risen by as much as 50 per cent. Sought-after areas such as Tuscany over the past

four years, and some beachside properties have almost doubled in price.

For many visitors the green hills and dales of Tuscany have proved irresistible. Sufficiently off the beaten track to ensure rural peace and quiet but easily accessible by road or rail.

Although land prices are no longer particularly cheap, buyers do get a lot of property for their money. Most homes have three or four bedrooms, large living room, spacious kitchen and bathroom, outhouses and up to ten acres of land.

Some of the best buys can be found nestling in hill-top villages, crowned with traditional pink-bricked buildings and winding cobbled streets. A substantial terraced house, with six inch thick walls and solid oak beams, paved courtyard in front and garden with fruit trees behind, will set you back around £40,000.

In Tuscany, a farmhouse on the hillside outside Florence, Sienna or Pisa provides the owner with a choice of views and the sea is barely an hour away by car. However, the closer to Florence, the pricier the property. The range for Tuscan property is £30,000 to £40,000 for a cottage in a pretty raw state, and from £80,000 to £150,000 for a sizeable abandoned farmhouses, ripe for renovation, standing in four acres of grounds in open countryside. Do check that consents have been given for the restoration work, before signing the agreement. In the green hills of Chianti country, at the region's heart, small-vineyards can still be snapped-up for less than £100,000. These usually include a derelict house, stable and outhouses.

A possible problem is water. Not all Tuscan properties have water and electricity laid on, and the nearest source of supply could be miles away, so it is worth checking that this necessity is easily and readily available at the outset.

The typical Tuscan farmhouse, stone-built with a red tiled roof, full of character, with big open fireplaces and magnificent arches, complete with a couple of acres of land, costs around £150,000. A similar property in the raw state would probably fetch around £70,000.

Umbria

Unlike Tuscany, now too pricey and well known for some British buyers, Umbria is an unexploited gem. Its soft rolling green landscape is sparcly populated with many isolated farms and villages now abandoned and in ruins. Until recently, Umbria was off-the-beaten track. Now, new motorways have opened in the Upper Tiber Valley area, and there is talk of upgrading the local Perugia airport to international status. Once that happens it will only be a matter of time before this peaceful region is firmly on the tourist map.

For the time being prices are still cheaper than those in Tuscany, although they are rising at the rate of 30 per cent a year, as buyers discover that Umbria is not only a pleasant place to live, but a potentially lucrative investment. As a holiday or retirement area few could do better. Its peaceful easy going rural lifestyle provides an alternative to the noisy nightlife and overcrowded beaches of the Mediterranean seaside resorts. It has fabled cities such as Assisi Gbio and its ancient capital, Perugia, steeped in art and history; with many a small church and local art gallery stiff with Renaissance masterpieces; and the ski slopes only an hour distant.

The characteristic old house have thick stone walls, rustic tiles and huge fireplaces. Many include the beautifully formed arches typical of the region. Also, as the world's finest marble is quarried nearby, the floor you walk on can be worth as much as the house itself. Prices range from as little as £15,000 for a tiny stone cottage set in an olive grove, without water and electricity and requiring extensive restoration, to about £200,000 for an abandoned medieval village.

A six-roomed hillside house, with four walls remaining and little else except fine views and fig trees, sells for about £30,000. A similar property fully restored with beamed ceilings and open stone fireplaces would fetch about £80,000. Roughly, £60,000 will buy an unconverted stone farmhouse, with up to eight rooms, and standing in a couple of acres of ground in open countryside. The top price of £170,000 will buy a restored eighteenth century villa with 20 rooms, frescos and marble staircases.

Some of the properties are on the edge of villages and easily accessible. Others are only reached by narrow dirt-track roads that snake, unnervingly high, up mountainsides. Many have no mains water, drainage or electricity, so it is important to check at the outset that this necessity is easily and readily available. Buyers should allow a sum equivalent to the purchase price to fund conversion from rural stone ruin to modern, sound, dry accommodation with kitchen and bath. For winter occupation some form of heating would also be necessary.

Several offerings in Tuscany and Umbria are on the books of regional specialists Italian Properties, based in Eckington, Worcs. Tel 0386 750133. Other agents include Italian Country Homes, Tunbridge Wells, Kent, Tel 0892 515611; and Brian A. French and Associates of Knaresborough, North Yorkshire.

The Italian Lakes

In the days of old when English aristocrats journeyed over treacherous Alpine passes, the Lakes were their first, unforgettable, sight of Italy.

Many stayed, and built their little whitewashed villas around their shores. Today, this enchanting lakeland district remains unspoilt. Here you will find some of the most exquisite villages in Europe. Some with tiny harbours on the lake, and others nestling amidst vineyards hung with great bunches of dark blue grapes.

The climate on the lakeshore is such that palm trees and almost every manner of fruit and vegetables, as well as a riot of flowers, will flourish at the water's edge. While, above the lakes, skiiers can practice their Alpine skills all-year-round, on the glaciers at an altitude of 3,353 metres.

Byron and Shelley wandered the wooded lakeshores, and scribbled a romantic line or two, Sir Winston Churchill put paint to canvas to capture a ravishing lakeside vista, and Queen Victoria stayed there – in an elegant lakeside residence, and the Italians responded to the honour by renaming the present hotel The Queen Victoria.

Until recent years, residential property for sale around the Italian Lakes, especially in sought-after areas around the famous Lakes; Como, Garda and Maggiore, was considered to be beyond the reach of the average British bank balance. Nowadays, other countries in Europe with more aggressively commercial holiday-home industries have long since overtaken the Italian lakes on the price scale. And, even if Como's famous villas, mostly owned by tyre manufacturers, are still worth a fortune, other less palatial homes do offer better value for money.

The selection of property available is considerable, both for newly built and resale homes, as well as a number of older properties that can be bought and converted into gems of tradition and comfort.

There are elegant lakeside apartments, honey-stone cottages, old timbered village houses, traditional beamed farmhouses and even magnificent old Renaissance villas, complete with a couple of frescos.

For the more intrepid, a ruined shell in a rural setting, with a stream, a well, a garden with peach trees, can still be found for about £15,000. But, you will need to spend at least another £15,000 to complete the necessary repairs and install a modern kitchen and bath.

For the skiing enthusiast who enjoys entertaining and doesn't mind mixing a little sand and cement, a rambling old mountainside house, already partially converted into a couple of self-contained cottages, on the edge of the slopes, can be found for around £50,000. Village properties are always popular here, and although prices tend to be on the high side in certain areas, there are still some good buys around.

A simple village house, close to the shores of Lake Maggiore, just two-up-and two-down, and totally unconverted will set you back round £20,000. A good quality renovation should fetch at least double that price.

A newly built apartment at Malcesine, set amidst the lemon groves, with a pool might appeal for use as a holiday home, priced around £50,000. This apartment is typical of the many well-designed clusters of flats built into the hillside above Lake Garda. Many apartments have delightful sun-terraces overlooking the lake.

Sardinia

The story of Sardinia's Costa Smerelda began 25 years ago when the young Aga Khan was persuaded by some friends in the banking world to invest $25,000 in buying 7,400 acres of rugged granite-backed coastline, sprinkled with silver sand coves, in the north-east of the island. Now 25 years and £450m later, the Costa Smerelda is a glittering dream world of lovely beaches, fabulous yachts, staggeringly expensive hotels, palatial villas and no sense of reality.

Centred on the yacht harbour of Puerto Cervo, where you could run into the King of Spain window shopping, all buildings are rustic in style, with walls as thick as oak trees, and not a new brick in sight to betray their youth. All new building is strictly controlled. No seaside building can exceed two storeys and none can take place within 160 yards of the beach, so villas built before this rule was introduced change hands for fortunes.

The cheapest seaside house costs at least £500,000 and £1m plus villas are not uncommon. There are however, a few less expensive properties. The development of Casa del Golf, on the slopes of the Pevero golf course, with views over the fairways to the sea, includes some two bedroom apartments costing from £180,000 for two bedrooms.

Villa building plots on half an acre or more, costing from £70,000 rising to £150,000, seem to offer the best value. Buyers should allow at least £250,000 for the actual construction, plus pool and landscaping, but no palm trees, because the Aga Khan thinks they are common.

The season is short in the Costa Smerelda – from June until late September, and jet-setters owning holiday-homes there take off for warmer climes during the winter months. The laws of mainland Italy apply in Sardinia.

Chapter Five:
SPAIN

The property slump in Britain has hit sales on the Spanish costas. Many thousands of Britains have used their homes in Britain as a source of money to buy Spanish holiday property. These have been used as security for loans to buy in Spain, or sold at a profit to buy a retirement villa abroad and a small home in Britain.

Controversy over the Ley de Costas – the Spanish coastal protection law – which has threatened some British and foreign-owned holiday homes built within 100–200 metres of the high-water mark, has contributed to sales resistance on the coast. Sales are slow, particularly on the Costa del Sol, which has traditionally been the most popular with the Brits. Cash buyers can easily negotiate 20 per cent off quoted prices on schemes where developers are badly extended and sales are geared primarily to the British. Better quality developments, with built-in sports facilities, such as golf, tennis and polo, aimed at a wider cross-section of the Euro-holiday-home-buying community, are less affected and prices are holding firm.

There is much more to Spain than just a handful of coastal resorts. Few of the crowds who flock to the three main tourist resorts – Costa Brava, Costa Blanca and Costa del Sol – venture into the hills behind. Yet to drive five miles or so into the mountain foothills above the noisy Mediterranean coast brings glimpses of life centuries old. Here you can find the real Spain, where the buildings give way to citrus groves, and where the business is still farming and not tourism.

Traditional Homes

If you are looking for a traditional home then Spain is an excellent choice with a range of locations, many a few miles inland from the Costa del Sol. Here you can still find the traditional Spain of the history books. The narrow cobbled streets, the ancient whitewalled buildings and the scent of the hibiscus. A simple terraced house, tiny and unconverted, can be yours for £25,000. A similar property, fully modernised, with walls as thick as oak trees, exposed beams and open fireplaces, would set you back around £50,000. Further up-market a three or four bedroom conversion with paved courtyard and peach trees flowering in the garden retails at about £80,000 to £100,000.

For those of you seeking something on a rather grander scale, £120,000 is the average price for a well-renovated Spanish hacienda. For this price you should have room for a handful of guests and a good couple of acres possibly planted with fruit trees out back.

The occasional deserted farmhouse, with a rambling old barn and well, does appear on the market. Prices depend mostly on the quality of the land in which it stands. A good starting price for a liveable place with essential services, i.e. water and electricity, plus a workable three acres, would be around £100,000.

A word of warning – buying wrecks and ruins is not for the faint hearted. There are a number of factors to be considered before giving full rein to a romantic notion of rural bliss in an isolated bolthole. The locals may be friendly, but you won't be able to communicate with them unless you speak Spanish. Security can be a problem if you live-off-the-beaten-track in Spain, and a car is essential, unless you plan to hibernate entirely.

There are a host of potential pitfalls associated with obtaining clear title to an older property, and without the advice of a good lawyer and thorough searches, you could find yourself in trouble. Homes in Mediterranean countries, like Spain, are often owned by several members of the same family, and getting agreement for a sale from each of the parties involved can be a long and difficult process.

Unlike buying a home in Britain, any debts outstanding on a Spanish property are inherited by the new owner. Unless these are revealed before you buy, you could end up having to pay the previous owner's unpaid taxes, building costs or community fees. You might even find there is a mortgage on your new home, which will need to be paid off before title deeds can be released.

Newly-Built and Resale Homes

Buyers are spoilt for choice as the property developers fall over themselves to erect homes along the various Costas. Competition is keen and the selection on offer can be bewildering. For instance a one-bedroom holiday flat in a fairly basic block in Benidorm set back from the sea can cost £18,000. A similar sized apartment on a beach front in a modern complex well served with swimming pool, bars, restaurants, shops and sporting facilities, could well cost double this figure at about £36,000. A more luxurious version located in a fashionable golf or marina complex may rise to four times the original sum i.e. £72,000.

The price of a villa can vary to just as great an extent. Key features being the exact location, quality of surrounding amenities and whether or not it has a sea view.

As a general rule of thumb new homes tend to be pricier than second hand. It's well worth checking out the resale market before committing yourself to a brand new place. Much depends upon your individual taste and priorities. For instance a holiday villa with two or three bedrooms surrounded by neatly manicured lawns in a densely populated resort of the Costa Brava may cost around £55,000. In comparison, a place of the same dimension in a new Costa del Sol development with twenty-four-hour security and lavish sports facilities, starts at around £120,000.

Costa Brava

There is renewed interest in the rugged north-eastern coastline, stretching from Port Bou on the Franco–Spanish border, to

28

the stamping ground of the beer and chips British holiday-maker. Behind it however, are small towns and villages in the Pyrenees foothills, reeking of history. Property prices have risen 30 per cent in a year, partly boosted by the Olympic Games to be held in Barcelona in 1992. There is little left for under £30,000, though you could buy an older off-centre studio in a tourist spot for around £16,000.

La Escala, a little town near the French border, will offer much more, with the atmospheric Greek and Roman ruins of Ampurias nearby and a construction ban on all sites of historic importance. The cheapest one bedroom flat costs about £30,000; two bedroom gardened villas start at £70,000 and detached houses about £100,000. It is about half an hour's drive from Gerona airport, or 12 hours by car from the French channel port of Calais.

Inland is Figueras, home of Salvador Dali's museum, and the peaceful medieval town of Pals, with its twisting cobbled streets and shady courtyards. The Catalonian countryside is scattered with quiet villages, many less than half an hour from the sea.

Property prices slip away from the coast, though values are rising. Those prepared to search some distance inland might find an unrestored rural stone house, with six rooms and grain loft, from around £40,000 (£80,000 nearer the coast). The fully renovated version sells for around £120,000. Agents: Woodside Europa, based at Bury St. Edmunds, in Suffolk.

If you want beaches and golf, there are housing develop-ments being built nearby Pals' 18-hole golf course, a chip and a putt from a secluded pine-trimmed beach. Golf Royale considered one of the smartest, where low-rise two-bedroom apartments start at £60,000. A detached villa overlooking the fairways costs about £160,000. Agents: IPI, based in Brighton.

Costa Blanca

Below the Costa Brava is the Costa Blanca. Winters are warmer and away from the coast there are towns and villages which have not changed for centuries. One hour's drive into the hills from Alicante, are old village houses overlooking the orange groves, with six rooms and crumbling stone walls, for around £30,000.

Prices of ruins are rising as buyers increasingly turn their backs on the coast, with its overcrowded beaches and high property prices, and head for the peace and tranquility of the hills. Restoration costs are high, but many of the derelict old farmhouses have masses of character and good potential. Avoid wrecks without water and electricity – cost of installation is exhorbitant.

Local agent Eduardo Van der Burg has a number of wrecks on his books. He recently joined forces with agents IPI, based in Brighton. Prices start at £20,000 for a land plot of half an acre and the shell of a farmhouse, with a well, but without water or electricity, some distance inland. The fully renovated version, with a few acres of workable farmland, sells for about £100,000. The average price is about £40,000 for a good-sized house with beamed ceilings and flagstone floors, in need of restoration.

Back on the coast, once-quaint towns like Benidorm, now lie buried under a sea of concrete and skyscraper blocks. Jarvea and Denia are among the seaside towns that always appeal to the British. The pace of life is leisurely, and climate and landscape ideally suited to retirement. Few high-rise blocks scar the landscape, most of the development along this stretch of coast consists of villas, built in traditional style, many with alcoves and arches formed in the local honey-coloured Tosca stone.

Both locations have strict conservation laws, which are pushing up property prices. Illegal sites of unauthorised building on cheap agricultural land are not unheard of in this part of Spain. The developer may hope to obtain planning consent after construction. If this is refused the buyer may be denied connection to water, electricity and gas supplies. So it is even more important to check that building licences and planning consents have been granted. Resale flats start at £30,000 for one bedroom, individual houses from £55,000.

Detached villas alongside the golf course at La Sella, near Denia, are selling from £90,000. One bedroom flats fetch

£40,000 and a two bedroom town house, with views over the fairways, costs £80,000.

Further south is La Manga, a skinny strip of land jutting out into the sea, once used as a military range, now covered with high-rise concrete blocks along the seashore. Nearby, on the mainland, is the 1,400 acre La Manga Estate. Bovis Abroad has taken over the task of developing this grand old colonial-style estate and golfer's haven, an hour an a half's drive south from Alicante. There are 3×18 hole golf courses, a plethora of tennis, squash and badminton courts and some 900 villas and apartments. Bovis is building another 1,300 homes as well as an extra 9-holes of golf. Price for a detached villa on the edge of a fairway: £280,000.

Costa del Sol
The 100-mile stretch of the Costa del Sol, from Sotogrande in the west to Montril in the east, with the city of Malaga as its focal point, is the most popular with sun-enthusiasts and property seekers alike. A rash of developments have sprawled across this stretch of southern Spain in the last 20 years attracting thousands of British holiday home buyers. In some new developments more than three-quarters of the buyers are British, paying anything from £30,000 to £500,000 for a place in the sun.

There is a glut of homes for sale with as much as £30,000 difference between two seemingly identical flats in neighbouring developments. Cash buyers are in the driving seat, prices can drop by thousands as you talk. Beware of cheap second-hand homes on the edge of a beach (the same applies elsewhere in Spain). These may be the subject of public enquries to decide whether or not they are built on the Spanish foreshore or within the protective band being drawn 100–700 metres behind the foreshore. The Shores Act 1988 gives the government the power to demolish properties built within this zone which were put up without planning permission. So, it's vital to check that all the necessary planning and building consents have been granted.

New developments close to Marbella, the social gluepot of

the Costa del Sol, start at £60,000 for a one bedroom flat. A newly-built two-bedroom town house will cost from £100, and a larger detached villa around £250,000. Marble floors, gold-plated taps and whirlpool baths are standard issue. You can have a more modestly priced piece of the Costa del Sol by picking an apartment at Hacienda Guadalupe, halfway between Marbella and Gibraltar, close to the small town of Manilva. Apartments set on a hillside overlooking the sea start at £37,000 for a one-bedroom flat. A four-bedroom semi-detached house costs from £100,000.

Another no-frills development is Arroyo Vaquero, near Estapona, where 100 Andalucian town houses are selling for between £75,000 and £95,000. Agents: Euro-Property Advisers, Salisbury, Wiltshire. If you want to buy British, housebuilder Lovell Homes is developing two sites on the Costa del Sol, one to attract the golfers, the other a traditional beachside location. At Pueblo Aida, a neo-Andalucian hillside village is being built. Traditional features include open fireplaces and oak beamed ceilings. Prices start at £80,000 for a two bedroom terraced house. Agents: Overseas Residential Properties.

The southern end of the cost, once rather remote, is now easy to travel to via Gibraltar. In the elite Sotogrande estate, with its 4,500 acres of grassland and golf courses, £280,000 will buy a four-bedroom tailor-made villa. Facilities include a school, church, doctor's surgery and a hotel. Sporting fanatics are well catered for with championship golf courses, tennis courts, riding stables, a polo ground, and a range of watersports. Nearby, a new commercial centre, incorporating a health and leisure club, has recently been completed. Sotoclub members, who pay an annual fee, can play squash, practice archery, go riding, join aerobics or dance classes. There is a gymnasium, indoor heated swimming pool, bar, restaurant and Members' Club lounge. Captain Mark Phillips is in charge of the Equestrian centre.

An apartment around Sotogrande's new port is a popular choice. Apartments at Puerto Sotogrande are built in grand style, many with massive sun terraces, enjoying fine views of the Rock of Gibraltar. The Harbour Village is built around the

550 berth marina. Two bedroom flats are from £125,000 and three bedders from £160,000. They are all on 75-year leases from the developer Puerto Sotogrande S.A. (3 Shepherd Market, London W1.)

Roads that snake their way up from the coast to hilltop towns, such as Rhonda, take you to a different world. Here ancient whitewalled houses line steep cobbled streets, and English is rarely spoken. Rural villages often offer better bargains than the crowded coastal belt, but be prepared to tramp around the countryside to find them. Agents, Fincasol specialise in finding old houses to restore.

At Benhavis, a few miles inland from the coast at Estapona, a replica of a medieval Andalucian vilage is being built. Misshapen old houses, with thick walls and studded oak doors, cluster around a cobbled square, with not a new brick in sight. Prices start at £25,000 for a tiny beamed one-bedroom flat, rising to £137,000 for a four-bedroom house, with original fireplaces, antique balconies and a roof terrace with views of the Rhonda mountains. The developer, David Marshall, is a local sculptor. Agents: Overseas Residential Properties.

Costa de la Luz

As the Costa del Sol reaches the province of Cadiz, it slips into the Costa de la Luz. The 'coast of the light' is that to the west of Gibraltar, its shores swept by the Atlantic ocean. Despite the opening of the border with Gibraltar, most of this coastline remains relatively inaccessible and largely untouched by development. However, with the Costa del Sol fast approaching saturation point in terms of construction, many developers are looking westward towards the Atlantic coast.

The Costa de la Luz will soon come into its own. Expo '92 – the biggest event to hit Southern Spain for 500 years – is to take place in Seville in 1992. Local infrastructure and communications are being improved in preparation for the 20 million visitors expected at the World Trade Fair. New roads and railways are being built, including a high-speed train that will link Seville with Madrid and the rest of Europe. Airports at Seville and Jerez are being improved.

Future development along this stretch of coastline will need to be carefully planned to protect the environment. The area abounds with nature reserves, including the 3,000 acre Icona Nature Reserve, south-east of Cadiz, and the 450 sq. mile Donana National Park, near the Portuguese border, Europe's biggest wildlife reserve.

The coastline west of Gibraltar has long been favoured by Spanish holidaymakers, though it remains to be discovered by mass tourism. However, several towns have already made their presence felt, including Tarifa, with its astonishingly wide sandy beaches, one of the windsurfing capitals of the world. In nearby Jerez, the sherry capital of Spain, a new holiday complex and marina has been built, alongside a swathe of sandy beach. At Puerto Sherry, Brent Walker, the international leisure group, chaired by George Walker, is developing an existing 1,000 berth marina, with dry dock facilities for 3,000 boats and 200 acres of land.

Brent Walker is building more than 1,000 homes and a £10m leisure complex with a five-star hotel, yacht club, a casino and a multi-screen cinema. Building is scheduled for completion in summer 1991. Many of the 750 apartments and town houses around the marina have been built and sold to Spanish residents, priced from £70,000 for a one bedroom flat. A further phase of 250 detached villas is planned alongside the new port.

Spain: There are two self-help groups for foreigners owning property in Spain. They provide information and offer advice to members in exchange for an annual fee.

International Property Owners, 72 Tottenham Court, London Tel 071-323-1223.

Instituto de Proprietarios Extranjeros SA (The Institute of Foreign Property Owners in Spain) 38 Hillfield Road, W. Hampstead, London NW6 IPZ. Tel 071-431-2499.

Chapter Six:
SPANISH ISLANDS

Canary Islands

Tenerife

Many Britons have bought a second nest in Spain's Canary Islands – seven specks scattered over 300 miles in the Atlantic Ocean, just off Africa's shoulder. Buyers have recently favoured Tenerife, the largest island, and their numbers are increasing. Aspiring property owners will find the island split in two by the 12,000ft volcano, Mount Teide, which makes for two quite distinct property markets. The north has luxuriant greenery, rain, historic villas and high prices. The south has year-round sunshine, and some of the cheapest property. For £25,000 you could pick up a one-bedroom flat.

A few years ago, an international airport was built in the south of the island and a new motorway constructed. Improved communications have led to a new resort at Playa de Las Americas and the expansion of Los Cristianos, a once-quaint fishing village, now buried under a sea of concrete. The development rate in the south is staggering, running at around 6,000 new beds a year, with plans for more accommodation and a new marina. Just ten years ago Playa de Las Americas was little more than scrubby desert, dotted with cacti and the odd mad, wild donkey. New huge hotels and apartment blocks proliferate, and massive signs announce 'exclusive urbanisations'.

Buyers are mainly British (more than 30,000 of them have set up home in Tenerife), paying anything from £20,000 to

£200,000 for a place in the sun. Property prices here are cheaper than those on the Costa del Sol and so is the cost of living with diesel at 80p a gallon and a litre of duty-free whisky costs under £5.

Tenerife benefits from a year-round holiday season, and many people have bought homes there with the intention of letting them as an investment. Now, good returns are only possible on top-quality developments with built in leisure facilities, such as golf. The recent fall-off in holiday bookings to the Canary Islands from the UK has affected letting.

Property prices have risen steadily over the past four years. However, the present glut of newly-built property is depressing the market in over-developed resorts, such as Playa de Las Americas. One bedroom apartments fetch from £20,000, two bedrooms from £30,000. Resale villas start at £85,000 rising to £200,000 for larger seafront homes.

One of the better new developments is Golf del Sur, a 'blue-chip' array of championship golf courses and low-density holiday villages, a chip and a putt away from the airport at Reina Sophia. Emphasis is on quality and space. Sports facilities abound and a commercial centre is nearing completion. Prices start at £29,000 for a studio apartment at Albatross Park, up to £110,000 for a two-bedroom two-bathroom villa at Los Cordones. All homes have marble flooring, satellite TV, wide terraces, residents' parking and some have private swimming pools. There are also landscaped gardens, fountains and waterfalls.

Many Britons are buying Canarian farmhouses and village houses complete with rustic balconies, beamed rooms and oak floors. Robin Broeckaert of local estate agents Castillo Sur says: 'Prices drop by around 300 per cent on the island as you move inland. You might get a land plot with a couple of acres and the shell of a farmhouse for as little as £20,000'. Broeckaert and his wife Hilda, have several properties on their books, priced between £20,000 and £80,000. Agents: Castillo Sur, Avd. Suecia 18, Los Cristianos 38650, S. Tenerife – Tel 010 3422 792319/292124.

Lanzarote

The most dramatic Canary island of all, Lanzarote, is perhaps one of the least known. Its fantastic lunar landscape of lava-encrusted mountains, fringed with almost shockingly white sand beaches, and its warm winter climate, provide the main tourist attractions. Despite the seemingly hostile environment – a pockmarked surface with over 300 volcanos – onions, tomatoes, melons and grapes spring in abundance from the black volcanic ash. The charcoal hillsides are pitted with rows of saucer-like hollows, half-ringed with low lava walls, to protect precious crops from the wind and to absorb and preserve moisture from the cool night air.

Lanzarote, together with its neighbour Fuerteventura, just 20 miles away by ferry (rather like a mini-Sahara and very popular with the Germans), has not been spared the abomination of modern Spanish development. Cheap hotels, slab-like concrete apartment blocks and low-cost timeshares, strung shoulder to shoulder along sections of the seashore. There are nicer parts, away from the discos and bars, mainly inland and at the more peaceful northern end of the island.

New development is supposed to be tightly controlled, although the amount of new building curently underway, much of it high-density, does not inspire confidence. There are some restrictions: you can paint the outer walls of buildings any colour you like – as long as it's white. The woodwork must be painted green or left with the natural grain. Otherwise boring, box-like houses are splashed with colour, with crimson and purple bougainvillea draped over whitewashed walls, and gardens with palms, geraniums, cacti, and poinsettias planted in the black picon ash.

New beachfront property is expensive. A seafront villa, close to a working fishing village, is likely to set you back at least £180,000 for three bedrooms. Of course, there are cheaper properties, in crowded beach resorts like Puerto del Carmen on the island's southern shore. The cheapest one-bedroom flat costs around £28,000 (resale) and villas fetch from around £60,000.

Property prices are more reasonable inland. The stark grey

hillsides are scattered with scrubbed white farmhouses, and on such a small island, none are very far from the sea. Here you could buy an old Canarian house, with open fireplaces, a wooden beamed inner courtyard, and at least ten rooms, for under £80,000.

Agents: Woodside Europa, Bury-St. Edmunds.

Gran Canaria

Despite its name, Gran Canaria is not the biggest of the islands, but its beaches are second to none. The coastline ranges from awe-inspiring cliffs to golden sand dunes. Inland, you can choose between stark mountains and tranquil valleys. The contrast of lifestyles is just as total. Travelling from the boisterous capital, Las Palmas, to one of the languorous provincial villages, is like abandoning Miami Beach for the Everglades. As the largest city in the Canaries, Las Palmas is more than just a provincial capital, it's a major commercial and historical centre, a cosmopolitan resort and a vital seaport, rolled into one.

The main highway south from Las Palmas speeds past mile after mile of desolate countryside all the way to San Agustina. Soon a rugged mountain range rises in the distance like a Western film set, and sure enough, many a low budget cowboy film has in fact been shot here. And then, out of nowhere, looms the overwhelming tourist complex of Playa del Ingles, a reincarnation of Miami beach in mid-Atlantic. Ten miles of golden beaches, backed by a new kind of boom-town sprawl — tall hotels, blocks of flats, bars, hamburger stands and shopping centres proliferate. While further on along the coastline the dunes of Maspalomas are large enough to constitute a local mini-Sahara. An oasis nearby relieves the blinding effect of seemingly endless white sand. Round the coast, beyond Maspalomas, smaller developments have been built or are planned for every promising cove.

You might find a small one-bedroom flat for about £18,000, or a bargain basement studio for as little as £12,000. The same size unit on a top quality new development will cost at least £30,000. A more spacious apartment, with two or three bedrooms, can cost from £35,000 to £100,000, depending on the resort and the standard of on-site facilities.

The Balearic Islands

Majorca

Majorca is the largest of Spain's Balearic Islands, and the traditional stamping ground of the beer and chips brigade of British holiday-maker. Less publicised are its residential charms; it is a surprisingly large island, with nearly 300 miles of coastline, much of it unspoiled, and a rustic interior where package tourists rarely venture, and which are now being explored by increasing numbers of prospective property buyers.

It is only the southern strip of the island that caters for the tourist trade, with high-rise hotels and cheap apartment blocks. Inland, there are high mountains, handsome villas, high prices and a colony of expatriates. A historic house, fully restored, set on a hillside with fine views and fig trees will set you back anything from £250,000 to over £500,000. Of course, there are some areas which are anything but delightful. But, prices are cheap, especially in densely populated districts around the capital Palma, where older off-centre studios change hands for less than £14,000 a time. A two-bedroom balconied flat can cost as little as £25,000 and a three-bedroom villa from £50,000.

On the other hand, there are a number of developments springing up on the island, with more than a touch of class. Apartments on the shore at Majorca's elite Anchorage club of Bendinat, along the coast from Palma, are selling from £120,000 for two bedrooms, rising to £250,000 for a penthouse. The Club, with its private pool, restaurant, library and piano bar, reeking of old money, is strictly members only, but residents are invited to join – for a fee. Inland, alongside the Royal Bendinat Golf Course (King Juan Carlos plays there) villa plots with a choice of designs and views around the bay, cost from £300,000 for a three-bedroom house and land.

Majorca is about the best of the Spanish Islands as far as

communications are concerned. It has an up-to-date telephone system and a good supply of direct dial lines. There are regular scheduled flights to most European cities throughout the year, with a number of cheap charter deals also on offer. On the down side, winter temperatures are decidedly cool, and when the weather hots up – so do the tourists. Permanent residents manage to freeze them out by living inland, or around a suitably snobby golf course.

Menorca

Unlike her popular sister island Majorca, Menorca is a tranquil laid-back island, with a rolling green landscape, rather like Devon, but without the rain. A patchwork of tiny fields, grazed by Friesian cows, bounded by thick hedges or drystone walls, scrubbed white farmhouses and peaceful villages. The island remains largely unspoilt by the over-development which has scarred so many Spanish resort areas. Therein lies its charm. Provided you enjoy the quiet life, Menorca is ideal – particularly for those considering retirement, and for families seeking a peaceful holiday home. The beaches are' perfect for children because of their long gentle slopes, lapped by waters as clear as a teardrop.

The island once belonged to the British and was only returned to Spain in 1802 in exchange for Gilbraltar. The British occupation left a legacy extending to Georgian architecture – with the only sash windows in Spain, and the 'boinda' (bow-window). It also left the locals with a taste for gin (still distilled on Menorca to this very day). It has been the chosen spot for a select set of property buyers for generations. Many of the Menorcan farmhouses are now British owned, and the supply of such properties in their unconverted state has virtually dried up. The first wave of British buyers are now being joined by a growing band of newcomers, attracted by the new residential estates springing up on the island.

Residential development in Menorca is low-key, and has so far largely been carefully controlled. Small cluster building is a feature of property developments on the island favoured by the planning authorities. One example of this is the Menorca Country Club, at Playa Fornells on the unspoilt north coast, where a range of villas and apartments is being built on a stretch of rocky coast, indented by narrow coves and swathes of sandy beach. Set in 65 clifftop hectares, planning permission has been given for an eventual 900 units, grouped around green zones and constructed in typical Menorcan style with whitewashed walls, rustic roof tiles, shuttered windows and moorish chimneys.

With stunning landscaping from three on-site nurseries, it is selling fast to British and Spanish buyers, (an encouraging percentage of owners are upwardly-mobile Spanish business-men) and prices are rising. Apartments with sea views, pergola and barbeque area on the terrace start at £38,000 and from £47,000 for two bedrooms. Garden villas with two and three bedrooms, are priced from £75,000, and detached villas from £200,000. Residents fork out a further £1,200 for membership of the club, with swimming pools, mini-golf, gymnasium, tennis courts, bar and restaurant. Agents/Developers: Menorca Country Club, Shepperton Marina, Felix Lane, Shepperton, Middx. (Tel 0932 243104 or 243168).

Ibiza
This is the most southerly of the Balearics, enjoys the best of the Mediterranean weather and is a firm favourite with the Germans and Scandinavians. It has been a hideaway for the rich and famous for years and has an active property market and a lively tourist trade. Ibiza, the capital, has expanded greatly in recent years, but the old town, built on a hill and crowned with a magnificent cathedral, has lost none of its charm. Although annual rainfall is low, the countryside is surprisingly green, watered with the help of numerous windmills, which draw their water from artesian wells.

The island is not without its share of over-development of the type that has blighted so many Spanish resort areas. The majority of building in recent years has been confined to areas around the tourist resort of San Antonio, and steps are now being taken to control the spread of unsightly development elsewhere on the island.

Santa Eulalia, to the north east of Ibiza town, is an attractive residential district with fine beaches and a selection of property under construction, including villas and apartments. Apartments range in price from around £40,000 for two bedrooms. Small bungalows and detached villas, with two and three bedrooms, cost from £55,000 to £120,000. Resale flats and villas in densely populated tourist spots can be found for a lot less, starting from £18,000 for a studio and from £40,000 for a small gardened villa. If you love wild parties, all-night discos and nude sunbathing, Ibiza is the place for you. If you don't, and you can't afford to buy a big enough villa far enough inland to escape such excesses – steer clear of this lively little island.

Agents: Associated Property International, 38 Queens Road, Brighton, Sussex.

Chapter Seven:
PORTUGAL

Portugal is coming into its own. Its landscape varies from fertile, wooded plains to high mountains with walnut, sweet chestnut and grape vines on the lower slopes. However, in contrast to Spain, her shores are swept by the Atlantic, which can produce uncertain weather. The south-facing, southern coastline, known as the Algarve, protected to some extent from the Atlantic gales, has attracted the majority of tourists and property speculators.

Originally colonised by the Romans, it was the Moors, in 711 AD, who swept across the sea from Africa and gave the Algarve its name, 'Al Gharb', from the Arabic meaning 'The Land in the West'. The moorish influence is still much in evidence today. Their distinctive style of architecture – low, cool white houses with fretwork chimneys have become the Algarve's trademark.

Disregarded for centuries by the Portuguese in the north, mainly because of its inaccessible and mountainous terrain, it was the British who thirty years ago rediscovered the area for tourism. Driving north from Gibraltar, as car passages became easier, some British families loved it so much they stayed and built white villas on its warm southerly hills.

Portugal's flirtation with revolution in 1974 may have been bloodless, but it did bleed the financial resources of many a developer at the time. Even some individuals lost home and money – property prices plummeted. Membership of the European Economic Community and a new centre-right Government, have both done their bit to bring new political stability to the country, and foreign investment is being actively encouraged. Now, the top leisure developments on the Algarve, and on the more northerly western coast around Estoril and Cascais, are again attracting top prices.

In the Quinta do Lago complex on the Algarve for instance, which has superb golf and tennis facilities, a three-bedroom detached villa could cost you £350,000. The same size property elsewhere would go for about half this sum. There is a wide range of holiday and retirement property on the Algarve. You can choose between a luxury villa with its own pool, a bungalow close to the beach, an old converted farmhouse, a traditional fisherman's cottage, and ultra modern golfing apartment, or even a converted windmill. Prices range from around £25,000 for a one bedroom flat in a run-down tourist block, rising to as much as £80,000 for the same sized flat in a luxury golfing development. Two bedrooms and sea views will set you back anything from £37,000. Terraced villas start at £50,000, and a detached three-bedroom, two-bathroom villa, complete with land around, can cost anything from £60,000 to £350,000 depending upon location.

New Development

Fortunately, a halt has now been called to the high rise developments of a few years ago. Recent changes in building regulations limit construction to a maximum of four-storeys, and density is being kept to a minimum. The planning authorities on the Algarve have finally woken up to the fact that unless they take steps to control the spread of unsightly development along their coastline, their future income from tourism will be seriously at risk.

It is too late for places like Albufeira, a once-quaint fishing village, now buried under a sea of concrete and skyscraper blocks. However, for the area west of Lagos and north from Cape St. Vincent to Aljezur, which were discovered later and remain unspoilt, the new regulations could mean that mistakes made elsewhere on this 100-mile Atlantic coastline will not be repeated.

The majority of upmarket housing is situated on large leisure estates, close to the international airport at Faro. Quinta do Lago is a good example of these potentially idyllic leisure developments. This is 'blue-chip' Algarve — 1,700 acres of rolling hills and pine woodlands, bordered by the Atlantic Ocean and the nature reserve of the Ria Formosa tidal inlet. More than 100 acres of fresh and salt water lakes form part of the landscaping, and to protect the natural beauty of the countryside, construction will follow the natural contours of the land; only 7 per cent will ever be covered by building.

Golf is the game here, with courses wall-to-wall — Quinta's 27-hole championship golf course, regular home of the Portuguese Open, has been joined by a further 18-hole course, and another nine-holes are on their way. There are also riding stables, tennis courts, sea-water lakes for windsurfing, restaurants, bars and even a nightclub.

There are already some very sexy villas on Quinta that would not look out of place in Hollywood or Beverley Hills, and the roll-call of owners reads like a 'Who's Who' in the City. Each villa is individually designed and surrounded by not less than half an acre, the building occupying no more than 20 per cent of the land. Villa building plots start at £175,000 for 2,000 sq. metres and an opulent four-bedroom house, with landscaped gardens and private pool, can be built for around £350,000, including the cost of the land. Owners must commence building within two years of purchase.

Existing holiday villages on Quinta do Lago, include Bovis Lakeside Village, overlooking the golf course and surrounding a fresh-water lagoon. Many of the 150 luxury apartments and houses have been sold to British buyers at prices from £110,000 for a one-bedroom flat, rising to as much as £280,000 for a detached villa with its own pool.

Just east of Portimao, but far enough west to escape the tourist hoards, Carvoeiro is becoming increasingly popular with investors who are prepared to drive an hour from the airport at Faro to find something special. Set in 40 clifftop hectares, a range of villas and apartments is being built on a stretch of rocky coastline, indented by narrow coves and swathes of sandy beach. The Carvoeiro Clube, not far from the fishing village of the same name, was started 20 years ago by the Moeller family from Hamburg. The original 150 acres is now fully developed, with stunning villas and an impressive sports complex.

A further 81 acres is now being developed with 120 huge villas, and the Clube's new 27-hole golf course is nearing completion. Prices start at £220,000 for a detached four-bedroom villa, sumptuously furnished, with large mature gardens and a secluded pool. Town houses and apartments are also available, some grouped around a replica of a traditional Portuguese village square, others set back overlooking the bay, priced from £60,000 for a one-bedroom flat.

The further west one goes towards Cape St. Vincent the scenery improves and property prices become more reasonable. There are very few existing high-rise blocks here, and much of the land is green-belt, which puts a stop to further building. Environmental protection begins just west of Lagos, where a preservation order has been placed on all beachside land, restricting future development; a stretch of around 40 miles, several kilometres deep, extending from Burgau to Cape St. Vincent and north to Aljezur.

Along the rocky coast road beyond Lagos, past vast deserted beaches, there are peaceful places still. Ancient white-walled villages like Burgau – a tiny gem, bright with flowers, where the business is still fishing and not tourism. Nestled snugly in the heart of the village, among centuries-old houses, the Vistamar and Tempomar apartments surround a pleasant pool. Many have private balconies and all enjoy restful views over the winding cobbled streets to the sea. These are available on a five year basis. Called 'Club 5', members are guaranteed holiday accommodation for the next five years from a starting price of £625 for a family of four. Apartments are fully furnished and equipped for self-catering, with daily maid service, however; there are no maintenance bills to pay.

A new 18-hole golf course has recently been completed close to Burgau, and this should help property values locally. The Parque de Floresta course, created by Pepe Gancedo, is the centrepiece of new residential and leisure complex. A village of just over 100 houses, grouped in small clusters around landscaped gardens and swimming pools, has recently been completed.

The two- and three-bedroom terraced houses, built in local style, with whitewashed walls and rustic roof tiles, are priced from £70,000. Villa plots are also available for homes built to individual specification. Prices start at £140,000 for a three-bedroom house and land. Facilities *promised* include tennis and squash courts, a fitness centre with sauna and whirlpool, and indoor and outdoor swimming pools, as well as bars, restaurants shops and a crèche. Agents: Europroperty Advisers, Salisbury.

Traditional Homes

Special care has to be taken when buying one of the many fine old country houses. Some still draw their water from ancient wells and may be many miles from the nearest electricity supply. Installation of essential services could cost a small fortune here.

Prices of traditional homes vary. If you are prepared to move some distance inland you can buy a ruined cottage with a couple of walls remaining for around £20,000. A converted country cottage, complete with garden with fruit trees and a few acres of land, would set you back about £40,000. For a traditional farmhouse, fully restored, plus a couple of acres of workable agricultural land, you will need to spend at least £80,000. A local agent with a good supply of country properties is Villas and Homes, with offices in the Algarve and in London.

Many Britons have chosen the Algarve for their retirement. The cost of living is no longer cheap; annual rates bills have risen steeply in the past year, and essentials, such as petrol, electricity and oil, are becoming increasingly expensive. Property rates are assessed once a year on the potential annual rentable value of your Portuguese home. So, a villa with a pool, at the edge of a beach or a golf course, (a lucrative letting option) will attract higher rates than a similar sized property, without a pool, situated some distance inland. Amounts differ widely, so it is important to check. The peak months for lettings are from the end of June until early October. Villas and apartments close to golf courses benefit from a year-round letting season.

Chapter Eight:
SWITZERLAND AND ANDORRA

Switzerland

Switzerland, land of sun, snow, mountains, gnomes and cuckoo clocks, has a lot going for it. Affluence, neutrality, economic stability, low taxes and one of the healthiest climates in the world – no wonder so many rich and famous people have set up home there. Many of those who have studied at Swiss finishing schools and colleges have enjoyed their early years in this mountainous country, and eventually retire as permanent residents.

It is not easy for foreigners to settle in Switzerland, and it is increasingly difficult to buy second homes there. There is a shortage of sites for building, due to the terrain, and the Swiss Government wants to prevent speculation. Indeed, in 1961 a ban was placed on the sale of property to outsiders. This has since been lifted, but the number of foreign buyers is still restricted.

The Swiss set an annual quota of sales. This was reduced from 2,000 properties in 1986 to 1,600 properties last year, and is likely to continue to fall. Only properties in a few provinces – or cantons, are authorised for sale, and usually only in tourist resorts. Homes in city centres like Berne and Geneva are banned, except to the Swiss.

There are also restrictions on the type of property available. Generally, foreigners may only buy newly-built homes (one per family), an apartment of less than 100 square metres, or a plot of land of no more than 1,000 square metres. Such properties are becoming scarce, and it is now difficult for an outsider to purchase an individual chalet.

Permission to buy property must be obtained from the local canton and from the central government in Berne. This process takes about eight weeks, and will usually only be refused if the foreign buyer already owns another home in Switzerland. Those fortunate enough to be allowed to buy their Swiss property, must not resell it for at least five years, and then only to a Swiss. After 10 years of ownership, or in the case of death, serious illness or financial hardship, it is possible to resell to a non-resident. Rules concerning resales vary from one canton to another, and in case of doubt the local notary will be able to advise you.

The Swiss impose certain other conditions on foreign property owners, but these are hardly onerous. There is an obligation for the owner or his family and friends to use the property for at least three weeks each year. Letting is restricted to a maximum of 11 months in any year, and homes can only be purchased in the name of an individual – not in the name of a company.

Owning a property in Switzerland does not confer the right to live there full-time, but it will help the owner to obtain a permanent residence permit. The Swiss are trying to limit any expansion of their 6½ million population, and rules about residence are very strict. You must be of retirement age, over 60, be sufficiently wealthy to be able to afford to live in Switzerland without working, and have family, friends or a home there. Most Britons who decide to buy property in Switzerland are looking for second or holiday homes, in which case they are permitted to reside for three months at any time and up to six months a year.

Annual maintenance costs on an apartment work out to around 1 per cent of the value of the property. This includes a contribution toward the reparation fund, buildings insurance, concierge, water, heating, snow clearance and upkeep of the garden. The owner also pays an annual property tax, plus taxes to the local commune, canton and central government, amounting to another 1 per cent of the purchase price. Death duties are payable in Switzerland, but these are much lower than in the UK, between 2 per cent and 7 per cent of the value of the property. If the property is registered in the name of more than one person, then tax would only be payable on the share of the property owned by the deceased.

Properties are not cheap. About £80,000 for a studio flat in a tourist resort is as low as they get. With more spacious accommodation, two- and three-bedroom chalet apartments near Montreaux or Lausanne could well cost from £200,000 to £400,000. Developments in ski-resorts and fringing lakes provide flats of various sizes from about £100,000 to £300,000.

The traditional Swiss 'chocolate box' chalet, window boxes bursting with geraniums, perched on a wooded hillside, with thick pine walls and a steeply sloping slate roof can be an individual home or an apartment building. Of course, there are other less attractive modern alpine buildings, but they are well insulated, often with triple glazing, and all have reinforced concrete cellars, with escape tunnels. These underground storage rooms are required by Swiss law for use in case of war as nuclear shelters, and must be supplied with water and provisions; enough, one assumes, for its occupants to survive the holocaust!

Many people prefer to buy a flat in an aparthotel to offset some of the costs involved in its upkeep by letting. The apartments are sold freehold, but the owner must allow the hotel to rent out his property (and his parking space) for a minimum period each year, usually about 150 days. The maximum period for letting is 250 days, and annual rental returns work out to about 3 per cent of property value. Such flats are often sold fully furnished, and have small kitchens for the exclusive use of owners. Prices start at £90,000 for a small one bedroom unit.

Most properties are available in the French-speaking part of Switzerland, particularly in the Canton of Vaud, in mountain resorts such as Villars and in the lakeside town of Montreaux. Some recently built chalets at Villars-sur-Ollon, a traditional Alpine village a few miles from Aigle, include one, two and three-bedroom apartments priced from £90,000 to £300,000. All have natural wood panelling in living areas, open-granite fireplaces, covered balconies and views of snow-capped peaks. There is underground car parking, laundry rooms, ski lockers and private cellars.

The chalets at Le Domaine de La Residence, a private 200 acre residential park, developed and maintained for over 30 years by Immobiliere Villars, are a short walk from the centre of the village and close to the little cog railway which carries skiers to the slopes of the Roc d'Orsay and Bretaye. There is a ski run which is used to ski back to the village.

The skiing areas of Villars are linked to les Alpes de Chaux, and to les Diablerets, with access by cable car to summer skiing on the glacier at 3,000 metres. Villars is a year-round resort, with over 120 km of skiing, 300 km of hiking trails, an 18-hole course, 20 tennis courts, an ice rink, several swimming pools, horse riding, paragliding and bowling. There are several restaurants, bars, tavernas, nightclubs and a cinema. It can be reached in just over an hour by car or train, from the international airport at Geneva.

Agents: Osbornes Solicitors handle a selection of property for sale in Switzerland: Osbornes, 93 Parkway, London NW1 7PP. Tel 071-485 8811. Also IPI, based in Brighton, Sussex.

Andorra

A tax-free haven nestling high in the Pyrenees, tucked away between France and Spain, undisturbed for centuries. That's Andorra with its population of 12,000 natives and 31,000 foreigners.

Duty free shopping, low density housing and a healthy year round climate combine to boost the country's attractions. The language is Catalan, the currency the Spanish peseta but the country is an independent republic with two co-princes outside its border, the President of France and a Spanish bishop. It is ruled by a twenty-eight-strong Andorran parliament and a handful of ministers.

Andorrans pay no income tax, have no diplomatic corps, no army, and just sixty policemen. The national income is raised from duty paid on imported goods, home-grown tobacco, cattle farming, and a vast emporium of tax-free shops, selling everything from calculators, cameras and computers to cigarettes, liquor, watches, perfume and jewellery.

Andorra has no currency of its own, and both the French franc and the Spanish peseta circulate freely, although the peseta is the preferred currency and all foreign exchange rates are quoted in it. Investments may be made and held in any principal world currency or combination of currencies, and can be switched freely to reflect moements in exchange rates. There is no minimum level for deposits, and bank accounts are confidential, with no disclosure.

Such fiscal freedom makes Andorra attractive as a property market, appealing to residents of high-tax countries who want to invest capital in a no-tax area, as well as to those who want a practical holiday-home with good capital-appreciation potential. There is more: for one other reason attracting buyers to Andorra is that it is a safe place to live, and one where outsiders are welcome. Added to this, the cost of living is relatively cheap, an estimated third below that of the United Kingdom.

Permanent residence is freely available to non-nationals, although work permits are rarely granted. The basic conditions include: ownership of property in Andorra, a suitable bank reference and a crime-free record. There are no special residential or financial qualifications for acquiring property, although no individual foreigner or married couple may have more than one residence in the Principality.

The capital Andorra La Vella is much like a mini-Hongkong, but within minutes of leaving it you are in another world. A world of beautiful valleys, studded with sturdy Alpine villages, and thick carpets of wild flowers on high pastures, which cascade in springtime in blazing torrents of yellow and blue.

Skiers who flock to the region in winter, to practice their Alpine skills, often return after the snows have melted to savour the delights of the countryside. In spring, summer and autumn, when the forests are brushed with gold, Andorra is at its best. Summertime temperatures soar into the 80°s and fall to many degrees below zero, when the snow starts to fall in early

December. Over the past ten years, several thousand British residents have enjoyed Andorra's stable economy. Property prices have been steadily rising since 1975.

The growing popularity of skiing boosts the investment value of land, houses and apartments, especially in the more accessible winter sports centres such as La Massana, north of the capital. Values are rising between 20 per cent and 25 per cent a year, with increasing demand for accommodation than can be let to tourists. Returns on rented property have breached the 10 per cent gross level and are still rising as building land becomes scarcer, and Andorra becomes more accessible to tourists.

Almost ninety per cent of Andorra's mountainous terrain is communally owned, and not available for sale or development. Of the remaining privately-owned sector, only a relatively small proportion of land changes hands each year, and prices are consequently high.

Development is tightly controlled by the Principality's government, which keeps a watchful eye on design and building standards. Traditional materials, including the use of local stone and slate, are required in construction. Regulations allow no apartment blocks to rise higher than six floors above the principal access. So, developers tend to build on steep slopes. You will often find buildings with two or three floors below road level and the maximum six above.

Most property is sold freehold, including apartments, in which case the owner takes a share of financial responsibility for the common parts of the block, expenditure on which is supervised by a committee of owners.

Less than a decade ago, derelict houses, wrecks and ruins, were thick on the ground. These days you'd be hard put to find the most humble 'borda' – the Andorran equivalent of an old barn, but bigger in area than a detached house – for much under £180,000. Everything was bought up and restored by the Andorrans themselves and a handful of 'canny' Brits, long ago.

New apartments vary widely in price depending upon location. A studio, in a traditional chalet style block, with a balcony and all modern conveniences can be found for around £28,000. One-bedroom apartments cost from around £35,000, and two- and three-bedrooms range in price from £45,000 to £100,000. At the top end come new luxury apartments in the sophisticated capital, Andorra la Vella, with two and three bedrooms, fetching £200,000.

One of the favourite areas chosen by many British residents is the valley and town of La Massana. It offers excellent walking and riding country, as well as fishing, tennis, squash and swimming in summertime. The Arinsal ski slopes are just five minutes away by car.

Cisa Andorran Properties, with offices in London and in the Principality, have built a number of top-quality developments here.

One of CISA's major developments, Anyos Park, 10 minutes drive from La Massana, has generated a tremendous amount of interest. The country club complex, built in traditional Alpine style, offers accommodation on an apart-hotel basis and has an extensive sports complex.

Anyos park nestles in a sunny Pyreneean valley, close to the ski-slopes, and each of the fifty-five studios and seventeen luxury one and two bedroom apartments, enjoy panoramic views of mountains and countryside. Facilities include: seven squash courts, four tennis courts two indoor), swimming pool, sauna, solarium whirlpool, billiards, rifle-range, snooker, gymnasium, satellite TV, maid service, crèche, restaurants, bar and transport to ski-slopes. Prices range from £28,000 for studios and from £50,000 for one and two-bedroom apartments.

The latest and most exclusive residential complex in the area, La Massana Park, is within walking distance of the village and 10 minutes from the ski-centres of Pal and Arinsal. Overlooking an unspoilt valley, the development will be set in extensive landscaping gardens. None of ·the properties are cheap. At the time of writing prices started at £111,200 for a one-bedroom flat, with marble floors, spacious sun terraces, video entry-phone and underground car parking.

High above the village of Arinsal, on the side of Pic Negre, with some of Andorra's best ski-runs right on the doorstep, the final phase of Edifici Amadeus is now available. The ground floor of the building comprises shopping arcades and a restaurant, and the 28 one-, two-, and three-bedroom apartments with stunning views of the valley below, are selling from £52,200.

There are a few cheaper properties in Andorra – at El Pedral, a new development alongside the new sports and leisure centre in Encamp, small furnished apartments, with satellite TV and telephone, start from as little as £30,000. Those seeking a more substantial family home might like a house at Bordes del Rutllan. Cleverly linked houses with large gardens and wonderful views overlooking La Massana valley are for sale priced from £160,000.

Cisa can also offer chalets and traditional-style 'bordas', designed by their own Andorran architects. These houses are built to the highest standards, and prices, including land, begin around £200,000.

New steps are being taken to improve Andorra's communications with the outside world, traditionally dependent on a three and a half hour drive along variable roads from Barcelona. A new Trans-Pyreneean Highway and road tunnel from Barcelona to Toulouse, passing close to Andorra, is scheduled for completion in 1990.

Andorra can be reached in two days, by car from England, with an overnights' stop in France. Airports: Seo de Urgel – just over the border in Spain, Barcelona, and Toulouse in France, Andorra also has its own airport, for light aircraft.

Chapter Nine:
GIBRALTAR AND MALTA

Gibraltar's famous Barbary apes are the symbol of UK sovereignty over the Rock. Legend warns that when the apes go the British will go too. However, there seems little danger of that: the apes are increasing in numbers – and so are the arrivals from the Old Country. The Union Jacks are flying, the policemen look like London bobbies and even the telephone boxes are painted red. There's fish and chips, Lipton's tea, and pubs serving British bitter. It's like London, but without the rain in this 2.25 sq mile piece of England tacked onto the Mediterranean coastline of Spain.

Finding an affordable place to live in such a small area can be a major problem; houses are like gold dust and freeholds as common as unicorns. The property market is limited as only around 5 per cent of the housing stock is owner-occupied. Thirty per cent is rented privately and the rest is let by the Gibraltar government.

Building costs are high compared with Spain, but this is partly because British building standards have to be achieved and what land there is costs more. Most of properties are sold leasehold, 99–149 years in length. A small leasehold flat (resale) without a fitted kitchen, can easily cost £80,000, and a turn-of-the-century terraced house around £250,000. However, because of the scarcity of property it does offer good capital appreciation and letting potential.

There is no capital gains or property taxes and no death duties. Exempt companies can be registered for a fee of

£225 and do not have to pay local taxes for a guaranteed 25-year period. There are no exchange controls; no double taxation agreements with any other country; and strict banking secrecy.

The reopening of the border with Spain in 1985 marked the end of a 16-year blockade when General Franco slammed shut the gates. It also heralded a new era for the Gibraltar property market, which had remained static during the siege. The growth of financial services in Gibraltar, coupled with an enormous increase in tourism, has led to a property boom. Rents are rising and prices have gained 30 per cent in the past year as banks, building societies, insurance companies, and all the other appendages of moneymen, scramble to set up shop – and home – on the Rock. The shortage of reasonably priced residential accommodation is a major worry for new arrivals. Apartments sell without a brick being laid, and rentable property is thin on the ground.

New property
Investment packages worth around £200m for new homes, marinas and hotels are to be put into operation and Gibraltar is sprouting skyscrapers, shopping centres, apartment blocks and multi-storey car parks. Developers from France, Spain and the U.K. are also investing heavily, and the increased yield from sales and rentals has attracted many familiar names.

A Taylor Woodrow project, Queensway Quay, has recently commenced on the Rock's western seafront. The £38m leisure development will incorporate 163 residential units, plus shops, a five-star hotel and casino built around a yacht marina, and will take five years to complete. An international hotel chain is negotiating to take over the hotel complex which will also offer conference facilities and a health club.

Much of the Rock is vertical so building land is limited. At the base of the Rock the city is crammed onto the sparce amount of flat land available. Modern developments, including new marinas, nibble into the sea. At Marina Bay, alongside the airport and overlooking the main runway, the harbour front is lined with luxury flats, offices, shops and restaurants.

Resale apartments appear on the market, priced from £85,000.

A new high-rise development on the western waterfront is the Watergardens, a £10m residential and commercial complex at Waterport Quay. Three 12-storey blocks, with 135 apartments and a commercial centre tower above the historic bay and another two blocks are planned. Balconied flats in the first phase, with views of sea and Rock, but without fitted kitchens, sold two years ago from £35,000 for a studio. The same unit today would re-sell for around £60,000.

Another new development, nearby the Rock Hotel and overlooking the Bay of Gibraltar, called Epram House will have 80 luxury flats and four penthouses. None of the apartments are cheap – prices range from £98,000 to £173,000 for a two bedroom duplex, rising to £250,000 to £300,000 for a four bedroom penthouse. But, residents are *promised* large landscaped gardens, video entry phones, underground car parking and a swimming pool (a rarity on the Rock).

A long term land reclaiming programme, planned and funded by the Gibraltar Government, allows for building three-quarters of a mile out into the sea. The Government is spending £5 million to reclaim 190,000 sq. metres of land, which it plans to sell to the private sector. This is intended to accommodate 1,500 residential units, an hotel and leisure complex, a private hospital and a 500 berth marina. The reclaimed land will increase the habitable space in Gibraltar by 40 per cent. The programme has already attracted considerable interest from around the world, including the Gibraltar government's latest deal with a Danish Consortium, led by the financial giant Baltica.

The Government is becoming increasingly aware of the need for adequate planning regulations. Height levels are being reduced and schemes that do not provide 75 per cent car parking are being rejected. Building on sites of historical importance is banned and new building in the old city centre must be designed to blend in with the surroundings. The Rock itself, with its 35 miles of underground tunnels, is crammed with military history, and the old town, with its tightly packed houses and narrow lanes, has lost none of its charm.

Traditional homes

Much of the architecture in the older parts of town, within the city walls, is an appealing mixture of English Regency and Italianate. The tall thin houses, with brightly coloured shutters and balconies in frilly ironwork, occasionally appear on the market, but prices are high and most would swallow another £50,000 on repairs. An elderly three-bedroom terraced in Governors Lane recently sold for £225,000 and an old fashioned four-bedroom family house in Cumberland Road, with roof garden, sold for £300,000. Agents: Trafalgar Property Services, Irishtown, Gibraltar.

There are three beaches scattered around the Rock, a couple of cinemas and a casino. If you want golf and horse-riding a trip over the border into Spain is necessary. There is a reciprocal health service agreement between Britain and Gibraltar, which is particularly useful for those considering retiring to the Rock.

GB Airways, Air Europe and British Airways all have daily scheduled flights to Gibraltar from Gatwick and Heathrow. Charter flights are also available from various operators. The journey takes about two hours and return fares cost from £120.

Malta

In Malta the natives speak a rather posh public school brand of English. It's as if the whole population had been educated at Eton – many of them undoubtedly have. The brave George Cross Island has many nostalgic reminders of Britain. They drive on the left hand side, swop war stories and drink beer with a pubby intensity.

It is a land of rugged charm. There are no rivers, no mountains, no lakes and not even a railway. The people are hospitable and friendly and the climate will warm the cockles of your heart. Temperatures soar into the 90°s in summer and rarely drop below 60°, even in the winter months. Many Britons choose this friendly former colony as a place to retire. The cost of living is amongst the lowest in Europe. There are no rates in Malta and the mild climate means hefty heating bills are simply a memory.

Malta is not so much an island as an extended group of honey-coloured villages. From the ancient hilltop city of Medina you can see stretched out before you nearly all of Malta. A patchwork of tiny fields, rubble walls, stone farmhouses, little churches and peaceful villages.

The rocky coastline, scattered with secluded beaches and limestone coves, is perfect for swimmers – with smooth rocks, bright sands and an unpolluted sea, as clear as a teardrop. Even in the tourist season, there are still places where your footprints will be the only ones in the sand, and there's plenty of opportunity to practice your aquatic skills. You can swim, sail or windsurf, go diving for octopus and crabs, water-ski or para-sail, or simply soak up the sun beside the still waters of Comino's vividly blue lagoon.

Getting about in Malta poses few problems. Inter-island ferries are cheap and the green Maltese buses may not be as distinctive as our red ones, but the prices are less flashy too. You can travel all over the island by bus for just a few pennies.

It has been a buyer's market for many years. Now a change of political direction has brought home-buyers back to this barren Mediterranean island and prices are starting to rise. Malta and smaller greener Gozo, offer a wide range of property, from converted farmhouses to modern flats and villas in Valetta or one of the outlying villages. Maltese people tend to have large families and this is reflected in the dimensions of the properties on offer. A 'modest' holiday flat, costing around £25,000 may have three or four bedrooms and often changes hands fully furnished.

For those with rather more to spend, a flat in an elegant mansion block, with caretaker, terraces and landscaped gardens surrounding a palm-fringed pool might cost around £40,000. Harbourside properties are particularly popular with those buyers considering permanent residence. Their proximity to Valetta, with its shopping and banking facilities, is a wintertime bonus. Prices are reasonable: £60,000 buys a newly-built waterfront penthouse, with three bedrooms.

You can find three-bedroomed furnished bungalows at the edge of a beach for as little as £45,000, and large detached houses, with marble floors and secluded gardens, from £100,000.

Rural retreats

To try and put a lid on property prices the Maltese government insists that foreigners cannot buy homes for less than £14,000. However, the occasional derelict house with well, minus mains water and electricity can be bought for less than this, provided enough money is spent on renovation to raise the price above this sum. Foreigners may not purchase a property which is deemed to be of significant historical interest, and an architect must examine any such home before an application to buy is accepted. However, Malta and Gozo are bristling with old houses, and only a few will come under this category.

Some of the island's best buys are to be found tucked away down the narrow winding lanes of the picturesque villages. Don't be put off by the bull's horn hung ominously from the front door – that's designed to ward off evil spirits not potential purchasers.

Many of these homes have leafy inner courtyards, tiny fountains and Italian style gardens. They do not appear regularly on the market but for the lucky few they can be bought and converted for around £60,000. Unconverted old Maltese mews houses are on the market for about £30,000.

A traditional stone farmhouse, with walls as thick as oak trees, but without water or electricity will set you back anything from £30,000 to £70,000, depending on the condition of the property and the amount of land involved.

For the really big spender, an exotic Roman style villa circa 1980, surrounded by vineyards and orchards, might be found for around £160,000. The property would typically include around twelve rooms, with Italian stained glass windows, being set in formal gardens with statues and fountains, with a shady vine-clad terrace overlooking the pool.

Local estate agent, Frank Salt (Real Estate) Limited, with two offices in Malta and another in Gozo, has a good selection of both newly-built and traditional homes on his books. Apart from selling and letting property, he also deals with property management and restoration.

Just one word of warning, water shortages can sometimes occur in densely populated areas. Many Maltese homes have working wells in the gardens, but it is important to ensure that a watertank for emergency supply is installed in the roof, before committing yourself to a purchase.

British residents are welcome in Malta, and people buying holiday homes may visit the island as often as they like. There are letting restrictions, although these have recently been lifted to allow foreigners owning villas with pools to rent them out. If your property does not fall into this category, however, you must not let it.

An application to buy property must be made in advance to the Ministry of Finance on the island and the permit is normally granted within three months from application. Foreigners may only own one property in Malta and Gozo.

Those considering retirement or making a more permanent home in Malta should apply for a permanent residence permit. The new permanent residency scheme is aimed at the higher income group and the tax concessions are favourable. A permit will be granted privided the applicant has an annual income of not less than Lm10,000 (£ sterling 17,200) or proven capital of Lm150,000 (£ sterling £258,000). This capital does not have to be brought into Malta, except for the amount needed to purchase a property.

The minimum income to be remitted annually to Malta is Lm6,000 for one person, plus Lm1,000 for each dependent, so a married couple would have to bring Lm7,000 (around £12,040) per year into the country. Applicants must either own a home on the island, valued at not less than Lm30,000 for a house, or Lm20,000 for a flat. He can also rent property of not less than Lm1,200 per annum (£1,500). In other words, a permanent resident is free to buy or rent a home, as he chooses.

There is a flat rate of tax at 15 per cent levied on all income brought into the island. Any unspent income or capital brought into Malta by the resident, may be repatriated, including the sale proceeds of any property. There is no capital gains tax in Malta so the full value of your property, can be transferred freely to the country of your choice.

Death duties are only payable on the deceased residents' Maltese estate, and no other assets will be assessed outside the island. Goods may be imported into the country duty free for the first six months of residency. Permanent residents are forbidden to seek employment on the island without prior permission from the authorities.

Maltese banks will lend money to foreigners wanting to buy property in Malta. Interest rates are fixed at 8%, and loans of up to 60% of the purchase price are available.

Charter flights are also available for independent travellers, through Intasun, direct to Malta from eleven UK airports. However, one could also drive down through Italy, and take the car ferry from Reggio, Calabria, Catania or Syracuse.

Chapter Ten:
CYPRUS AND TURKEY

Cyprus
This former British colony still reserves a warm welcome for people from the 'old country'. Nearly everyone speaks English, they drive on the left hand side of the road and their telephone boxes are painted red. Cyprus has 340 days of sunshine every year, a sea temperature which never drops below 60° Fahrenheit, cool pine clad mountains and fine sandy beaches.

The timeless Cyprus charm captures you with brilliant bougainvillea, hibiscus, lush orange and lemon groves, and grape vines heavy with deep purple fruit. And, only in Cyprus, will you see a road sign warning: 'Caution: Road slippery with grape juice!' Today, Cyprus maintains its tradition of hospitality. In the countryside villagers shyly sidle up to you with invitations to their homes. This is not a thing to be missed – stuffed with baked lamb and drowned with Cyprus brandy, you stagger out, into the dazzling sunshine.

On the narrow cobbled streets of the whitewashed villages, nut-brown old ladies sun themselves at cottage doorways. While they make their delicate lace, their husbands seem to have endless time to pass in the coffee shops, sipping ouzo and playing dice.

The courage of these hospitable people cannot fail to impress. After losing a third of their island to the Turkish years ago, they have since developed the holiday resorts on the south coast and are now keen to attract overseas property buyers.

In addition to the many British servicemen still in Cyprus, there are around 3,000 permanent British residents and several thousand more Britons own holiday homes there. Income tax is low and the cost of living, although rising, is among the cheapest in Europe, as is the cost of housing. However, a new rule prevents foreigners from letting their property in Cyprus.

The selection of property available in Cyprus ranges from wrecks and ruins, to newly-built luxury, bordering on opulence. Take your pick from a traditional village house, a tottering taverna, or a rural stone cottage on a mountainside. There are neat white holiday villas and apartments at the edge of a beach, and magnificent Mediterranean-style villas, with sun-terraces, pools and fountains, nestling in splendid isolation on remote, olive-clad hillsides.

Traditional homes

There are restrictions on the amount of land that foreigners can buy in Cyprus. Currently, around two 'donums', almost an acre. This, sadly, rules out the avocado farms and ancient vineyards, which many British buyers often seek out. However, there are plenty of derelict village houses, with pleasant leafy gardens, to be found in the midst of lemon groves.

Mountainside cottages, overgrown with olive trees, often draw their water from ancient wells, and many have traditional bread-ovens in the gardens. Prices are nearly always 'by negotiation', and therefore precise valuations are difficult.

However, a tumble-down ruin, in a rural setting, can be found for as little as £10,000 – that's if the owner takes a liking to you. If he doesn't, he probably won't sell you the place anyway. Installation of essential services, i.e. water and electricity, can prove expensive here, so do allow a sizeable financial cushion for this. You will have to pay roughly twice this for a white-washed village house partially converted with a modern kitchen and bathroom.

Local estate agents specialising in traditional homes are thin on the ground and you will not find big 'For Sale' signs to tempt you. A local lawyer often will seek out what you want, and bargain in the traditional manner. Bargaining is a delicate art in Cyprus, and the uninitiated will almost certainly pay over the odds.

New property
Despite the various architectural scars, sky-scraper blocks and so on, that have been built around Larnaca and Limassol, fortunately some attempt has now been made to keep the concrete cowboys at bay. Recent changes in planning laws limit buildings to four storeys in height, and construction, on sites of historic importance, is strictly prohibited.

Around Paphos, where it is almost impossible to put a spade in the ground without striking some archaelogical artifact, development has come to a virtual halt and building density is at a minimum. A local vigilante group of conservationists keep an eagle-eye on the developers, just to make sure they conform with the rules!

Paphos, where a new airport has recently been completed, is in the south-east of the island. It is a picturesque old harbour town, famed for its beautiful mosaics and ancient Greek and Roman remains. The surrounding area has some of the island's better beaches and the soaring Troodus mountains nearby enable residents to ski and swim, in the same day.

You can still buy a small second-hand studio near Paphos for as little as £16,000. A one-bedroom flat starts at £22,000, a two-bedroom one from £28,000 and the larger three bed-room units sell for £50,000. Prices of newly-built villas range from £40,000 for a small two-bedroom house, some distance inland, rising to about £60,000 for a similarly-sized seaside house, and from £100,000 for a large detached house, with landscaped gardens and sea views.

Leptos Estates is a successful developer in the Paphos area and has been building homes in Cyprus and the Middle East for more than 25 years. The developer also has a London office. Its development at Paphos Gardens has proved particu-larly popular with British buyers.

Close to the sea, and ideal for families with children, Paphos Gardens consists of clusters of low whitewashed villas, built in local style. The surrounding gardens are positively sub-tropical, and amenities include swimming pools, restaurants, shops and tennis courts. Resale studios occasionally appear on the market at £19,000, one-bedroom apartments retail at around £28,000, and the price of a two-bedroom maisonette rises to £50,000.

Those seeking a more permanent home, with eventual retirement in mind, might prefer a newly-built villa in Stephanie Village. This consists of two groups of fifty villas, divided by an ancient vineyard, a mile or so inland from Paphos. Prices begin at £57,000 for a detached house with two large bedrooms and well-stocked gardens back and front.

Close to the foothills of the Troodos mountains and over-looking the Bay of Paphos, is the newly-created village of Kamares. The name means arches and there is plenty of evidence to underline this. Only around half of the total area is designated as building land with villas of one or two storeys on plots of between 800 and 12,000 square metres. Trees and shrubs have been carefully preserved in a massive landscaping programme, and extensive use is made in construction of the local honey-coloured stone.

Villas are built in grand style with huge sun terraces, patios and private pools and all have stunning views over the mountains to the sea. All the properties are detached and prices start at £50,000 for a two-bedroom villa, while those with four bedrooms, ensuite bathrooms, and a private pool cost closer to £100,000.

None of the properties on this development are small, and the peaceful environment makes them ideally suited for permanent homes, although a car is a necessity here. Owners have the use of the Kamares Club-house. Amenities include a restaurant, bar, games room and swimming pool. The best villas and apartments in each development hold their values well, but still take up to six months to resell. In the past two years the resale market has been depressed by a glut of Arab resales.

Rates, charged by local authorities in the United Kingdom, are unheard of in Cyprus. However, owners have to pay separately for services such as refuse collection, septic tank emptying and mains water. This works out to around £360 a year for most households.

Before buying a home in Cyprus, application must be made to the Council of Ministers on the island. For permanent residency you must apply to the District Officer in the chosen area. Permission is granted as long as you can provide proof that you are self-supporting. For those retiring to Cyprus, there is a minimum income qualification of around C£3,000 for a single person and C£4,500 for a married couple.

Turkey

If Turkey today wakes to the rhythmical wailing of the first call to prayer, an hour before dawn, then Turkey tomorrow will rise to a chorus of sledgehammers, pneumatic drills and concrete mixers. It is not quite the Costa del Sol yet, but the babble of English in the bazaars is growing. British tourists are switching from Sangria and sombreros on the Spanish Costas, to silk carpets, steam baths and a taste of Turkish hospitality.

Last year 45,000 Britons visited Turkey, compared with only 9,000 in 1986, and this year that figure could double. As the Turkish government has designated large slices of its Aegean and Mediterranean coasts as prime tourist development areas, the property market is bound to follow in the footsteps of the country's holiday industry.

Foreign investment is being actively encouraged. So far Turkey shows little sign of having learnt from the experiences of Spain and other countries, and the projected development rate, coupled with the slab-like hotels and apartment blocks springing up around Marmarais, one of the country's best known resorts, do not hold out much hope. Fortunately, some attempt is being made to restrain the concrete cowboys. This is particularly evident around Bodrum, an historic harbour town, set in a sheltered bay on the peaceful south-west coast. It is growing at the rate of 1,000 tourist beds a year, from an existing 10,000 up to a planned 40,000, but does not intend to sacrifice the environment.

Building regulations limit construction to a maximum of three storeys, and the authorities are very strict about density.

Penalties for law-breakers are severe, as a local builder who disregarded the rules discovered when the army moved in with their bulldozers.

The British are allowed to buy freehold property in Turkey, but only within large towns or municipal areas, to prevent prices in rural areas rising beyond the reach of local people. Laws rule out the converted shepherd's huts or derelict village houses which so many Britons seek out. The situation could change, given Turkey's application for full membership of the European Economic Community.

There is plenty of property for sale, but you will not find big 'For Sale' boards or local estate agents' particulars on hand. However, there are a number of estate agents in this country who handle Turkish property in association with Turkish agents and developers. Information is best gained from the Turkish Embassy in London, or from a visit to the country.

Prices are nearly always '*by negotiation*', and can drop by thousands as you talk. An alternative is to shelter behind a local lawyer who will seek out what you want, and bargain in the traditional manner. It is a skilled art in Turkey, and the uninitiated will almost certainly pay over the odds.

The Turks are friendly and hospitable (English is spoken widely in areas frequented by tourists) and foreign settlers are welcomed. Property is cheap, as is the cost of living, though prices are rising rapidly in some holiday resorts.

Allow at least four hours to drive from Izmir airport to Bodrum. A new airport is planned just 30 minutes from the town; its completion would help boost local property values.

Bodrum is a fascinating old town with a bustling harbour-front and an impressive crusader castle. Local restaurants serving charcoal grilled fish and meats, offer excellent value and in the bazaar you can buy everything from exotic spices, to fake Lacoste tee-shirts, fur coats and Turkish carpets. The beaches are rather narrow and shingly, so people swim from wooden jetties. Property prices range from around £12,000 for a one-bedroom flat (resale), rising to £80,000–£100,000 for a newly-built six-bedroomed villa, with land around.

British overseas property agents Tavnerstar, based at Kingston-upon-Thames in Surrey, in association with Turkish agents Pozcu & Collard, represent seven developers active in the Bodrum area. They offer a wide selection of newly-built homes on a number of developments, priced from £16,500. These include two- and three-storey terraced town houses, built in local style, with whitewashed walls, wooden shutters and flat sun roofs. All have balconies or terraces, overlooking a palm-fringed pool and beautifully exotic gardens, just a few minutes walk from the centre of Bodrum.

There are also some large and opulent seafront villas on developments with leisure facilities that include a marina, helicopter pad, indoor and outdoor pools, a fitness centre and tennis courts. Prices (inclusive of registration and notary fees) start from £16,500 for a one bedroom balconied flat, rising to £100,000 for a detached house, with at least six bedrooms, private pool, and landscaped gardens dotted with date palms.

Both freehold and leasehold properties are available. In the case of leaseholds, the solidity of a lease is guaranteed by a Turkish bank. The Yapi Credit Bank – one of the big three Turkish banks – buys the freehold on the villa or apartment, and offers the foreign purchaser a 999 year lease on the property.

Rentable holiday property is thin on the ground, so returns are good: from around £160 to £180 per week, depending on size and season. That income would be taxed at 20.6 per cent (although, holiday rentals organised in the UK would be beyond the reach of Turkish tax officials).

Some of the laws relating to property are a little quaint, and trust plays an important part in any transaction. However, it is early days yet in a country where a typical property transaction is sealed with the buyer and seller shaking hands and taking off for the land registry. It can get very hot in southern Turkey, and distances can prove longer than expected. The countryside is rich and varied, and with the treasures of successive generations strewn across Anatolia, effort spent will be well rewarded.

Further information about buying property in Turkey can be obtained from Hayrettin Uzun, financial and customs counsellor, at the Turkish Embassy in London.

Chapter Eleven:
EXOTIC ISLANDS

The Bahamas

The Bahamas, including the two main centres of Nassau (New Providence) and Freeport (Grand Bahama) and 700 outer islands, mostly uninhabited, are scattered across some 100,000 square miles of sea off Florida's shoulder. The two main islands have sizeable British and American expatriate communities. People living on the Bahamas enjoy tremendous tax advantages. No taxes on capital, income, profits, inheritance or dividends exist. Proven financial security is required of those seeking residence, although there is no minimum rule on income. Those who wish to reside for more than eight months will be charged an annual fee of $1,000 with a further 20 dollars for each dependent. Britons seeking permanent residence will be charged a once-only fee of B$5000.

However, property is expensive here. Nassau, the capital has expanded in recent years and many new holiday flats, beachside apartments and luxury villas have been built. An apartment might be found for under US$150,000, but the majority cost a great deal more. Cheaper properties can be found on isles along the outer rim, like Andros, Exhuma and Abaco. The best house sites are not by the beach, but on higher elevations. The same holds true for many other Caribbean islands.

An application to buy property must be made to the Foreign Investment Board in Nassau who will issue the necessary permission. This is to prevent speculation and is merely a formality. The Bahamian economy is based on the US economy and costs are roughly comparable, although local produce is plentiful and cheap. The islands are best enjoyed during the British winter months when the climate is more forgiving. Agents: Smith Gore, London.

Bermuda

Bermuda is Britain's oldest self-governing colony, where the beaches are stunning, the sea is warm and blue, and the best of British still applies: old fashioned courtesy and good manners. Perfect strangers smile and say 'good morning' and 'have a nice day'. There are no hire cars and only one car per household, everyone drives on the left and the slow-moving traffic – speed limit 20 miles an hour – is directed by bobbies in British helmets . . . and Bermuda shorts.

The whole place is squeaky clean, slow, safe and pretty. Dainty pink and white cottage colonies, their coral rooftops dazzling in the bright sunlight, scattered around emerald and sapphire waters, between manicured golf courses, big hotels and millionaires' homes. There is no poverty, no slums, no dirt, no unemployment and no income tax. No wonder the rich are so at home there.

Bermuda is a little place, a mere 20 miles long and less than two miles wide, a string of tiny coral islands linked by bridges or causeways into one small but beautiful country. It is NOT in the Caribbean, which lies 1,000 miles south. It is 600 miles out in the Atlantic, off North Carolina, but because of the warm embrace of the Gulf Stream it has a warm sub-tropical climate.

Bermuda enjoys one of the highest per capita incomes in the world. All the food, clothing and appliances have to be imported, and the cost of living is high. New settlers are welcomed, as long as they are respectable and above all rich. For Bermuda operates a two-tier property system to preserve affordable homes for residents, based on an annual rental value put on each house. Foreigners cannot buy any house with an annual rental value below BE$37,000, or an apartment below BE$13,200. This rules out any house worth less than BE$80,000 or any flat under BE$300,000.

Not that there are many properties available below that price floor. The most palatial homes go for a great deal more. In prime residential areas like Tuckers Town, where a large and luxurious summer house is likely to have its own lagoon, private beach, two guest houses, tennis court and citrus grove. Worth at least BE$10 million, these are strictly for millionaires. At the other end of the scale you could buy a three-bedroom beach condominium, with a view over Harrington Sound, for BE$500,000. There are a few cheaper 'condos', many on the edge of a pink coral beach, selling for around BE$350,000 for two bedrooms.

Having found a property that qualifies, you must then gain permission from the Bermudian Government. It takes around four months before a licence is granted. All property is subject to an annual land tax of at least BE$2,200 for a house in the non-Bermudian price bracket, and around BE$1,200 for a condominium. No foreigner can buy more than one property on the island.

British Airways operate five flights a week to the island from Heathrow and the flight takes seven hours. Further information can be obtained from Bermuda Tourism, 6 Burnsall Street, London SW3 Tel 071-734 8813.

Caribbean

The Caribbean islands have long been popular haunts with British and American buyers in search of a home on a tropical island. Although house prices have remained static in recent years, high levels of tourism in many islands have renewed interest in the property market, creating greater activity and causing values to rise. However, the recent hurricane (the worst this century), has affected prices, particularly in the Cayman Islands, Jamaica and St. Lucia, parts of which were devastated by the high winds.

British Virgin Islands
Hurricanes hardly ever happen in the British Virgin Islands. Located around 100 kms east of Puerto Rico, the islands have a favourable sub-tropical climate, without undue extremes of heat or humidity. Many of them are mountainous, and of the 40 or so islands, only 15 are inhabited. The largest Tortola, where the capital Road Town is situated, is the financial and

administrative centre, and where the main shops, banks and hospitals are located.

Due to its close proximity to the US, many expatriates are from North America. The status of British colony has, for many years, also attracted many Britons, and there is a sizeable rentable value. A tax-free break of up to 10 years is offered to businesses which are deemed necessary in the islands.

Visitors from the UK may stay for up to six months, provided they can prove adequate means of support and hold return tickets and pre-booked accommodation. Those wishing to take up residence or invest in the islands should contact the Chief Immigration Officer on Tortola. Health facilities are reasonable, but private medical insurance is essential, as it is in any of the Caribbean islands. Agents: Smith Gore, London.

Barbados

Further south and east, Barbados continues to attract strong interest from the British. The perfect climate and welcoming people are obvious attractions of this 166 square mile coral island, swathed in sugar cane, and blessed with some of the finest white sandy beaches anywhere in the Caribbean. But, what sustains the continuing interest of both European and US investors is its economic and political stability.

Here a favourable tax structure is the major attraction for investors. There is no wealth tax, death duties, or capital gains tax. Income tax is charged on income held by individuals in accounts elsewhere in the world, on a sliding scale between 5–20 per cent. Foreigners or 'non-belongers' are free to buy property and live on the islands provided they can prove adequate means of support. Here a palatial four-bedroom home, can be built to your own specification on a first class site, for around £100,000.

Several new housing developments, on a more modest scale, are being built on Tortola, including villas on plots of around an acre and some apartments at the water's edge. Private land can be leased or bought for development by obtaining a landholding licence. In the case of foreigners buying land this must be built on within two years to prevent speculation.

Tax on land for 'non-belongers', is around US$20 per year for the first acre, and around US$10 thereafter. A property tax of 1½ per cent is levied on all privately owned buildings.

Barbadians are governed by the third oldest democracy in the Commonwealth, the first parliament sat there in 1939. It is a civilised and well-ordered island, with its bustling capital Bridgetown, supported by good public utilities and excellent communications. There are international flights daily.

Despite its popularity with Americans, Barbados still maintains its British atmosphere and the names of its villages make the English expatriate feel at home – Hastings, Brighton and Worthing – and there is even a Nelson's Column and Trafalgar Square. There are a number of long-established British residents, whose families have owned homes there for generations.

House prices have been static in recent years, but agents are now reporting increased activity, accompanied by a steady growth in values. The Barbados dollar is geared two-to-one directly to the US dollar, although house prices are generally quoted in US dollars. Added encouragment is given to investors by the beneficial tax arrangements. There are no death duties or capital gains tax, and the government gives incentives for hotel development, by means of tax exemption on profits over a 10-year period.

However, unlike similar islands, Barbados is no tax-haven. Tax on income is levied, and although there are no restrictions on foreigners buying property a purchase tax of 17 per cent is incurred, plus legal fees.

Individual villas and historic plantation houses are for sale all over the island, but one of the more popular new developments is at Glitter Bay. Although it is still possible to find a furnished house or apartment for under £50,000, most cost a great deal more. These are mainly individual villas, usually built to order and often on an opulent scale.

For about £120,000 you could be the proud owner of a two-storey 'Hacienda-style' courtyard house, with four bedrooms and staff quarters, surrounded by exotic gardens that sweep down to the sea. A palladian-style plantation house, surrounded by manicured lawns extending to three acres, with panoramic views, large swimming pool and guest cottage in the grounds, recently sold for about £1m. Agents: Smith Gore, London.

The Cayman Islands
The three Cayman islands, Grand Cayman, Cayman Brac and Little Cayman, step down in size and in population, together covering some 100 square miles, almost 500 miles south of Miami. The capital George Town is situated on the largest island, Grand Cayman, with a population of over 4,000 people. About 2,000 live on Cayman Brac and less than 100 people on Little Cayman.

In contrast to most Caribbean islands, the Caymans are quite flat. However, their beaches are superb, and there are some beautiful underwater coral reefs. Anyone who loves swimming, sailing, fishing or scubadiving in crystal clear waters, but hates taxes, will love the Cayman Islands. There is no income tax, corporation, inheritance, capital gains, wealth, sales or any kind of tax imposed. However, property is not cheap. A small apartment will cost at least US$150,000 and detached houses fetch anything from US$350,000 up. A list of estate agents may be obtained from the Cayman Islands Government Office.

The status of this island group as a British colony continues to attract a number of British expatriates. Those seeking permanent residence should contact the Chief Immigration Officer on Grand Cayman. Prospective residents have to prove sufficient financial means, and to invest a minimum of CI$150,000 in the islands. Non-residents have to obtain a work permit before seeking employment.

Hurricanes in the Caribbean hardly ever happen, but when they do sweep past the Cayman Islands, serious damage can occur. However, the usual climate of these idyllic isles is perfect year-round, without extremes of heat or humidity. The cost of living is high, compared with Europe. Most goods need to be imported. Communications are good for such a small country. Cayman Airways run twice-daily services to Miami and five times a week to Houston. There is also a service operated by Air Jamaica which flies to the island three times a week.

77

Chapter Twelve:
FAR AWAY PLACES

Australia

Despite its vast size and huge variety of scenery and climate, entry into Australia isn't easy. Those wanting to live and work there must have a skill or talent which is going to benefit their new host – or a close relative who will sponsor them. Anyone contemplating retirement can apply for permission to go and live there, provided they have a good character and are in good health – and an income of no less than $A400 (about £200 a week).

There are no restrictions on foreigners buying property, although it's a long way to go for a holiday home! There are some apartment blocks and town houses, but the typical Australian dwelling remains a single-storey house on a large plot of at least a quarter of an acre.

Property prices are rising. These days it is difficult to get a waterfront house in Sydney (certainly, the most expensive place to buy a house in Australia) for under £250,000. A similar property, in one of the coastal suburbs such as Bondi or Manly Beach, (second or third line) consisting of three bedrooms with 'built-ins', 'eat-in' kitchen, vast sundrenched living area and a 'rumpus' (family) room, on a third of an acre plot, could be found for around £60,000.

An air-conditioned apartment in the heart of Sydney, with three bedrooms and ensuite baths, designer kitchen and two reception rooms, plus sun-terraces and underground car parking, would set you back the same sort of money. Most homes are fitted with high-tec security systems, at least one double garage, and kitchens come fully equipped down to fridge freezers, dish-washers, and microwave ovens.

Prices are cheaper in Perth, western Australia – and the weather is better. The country's fastest growing city benefits from a year-round Mediterranean climate. On the banks of the Swan River (so vast it makes the River Thames look like a stream), not far from the Royal Perth Yacht Club, £150,000 buys a large opulent house with four double bedrooms, lavish bathrooms, a study, formal dining room and large family room, gourmet kitchen and double garage. And, of course, no home in Perth is complete without a swimming pool, palm trees and a boat house (one in every three citizens own their own boat). Agents: OPB Ltd, Penn, Buckinghamshire.

Canada

High standards of living are enjoyed by almost all, due to the low level of inflation and high wages. The cost of living is higher than in the UK; the cold winter climate means heavy winter heating bills. Capital gains tax on 50 per cent of capital gains on all assets (except one principal residence) is chargeable as part of the income. Income from all sources in or outside the country is subject to federal and provincial tax after specified allowances.

You can go and live in Canada, provided you are over 55 years old, have sufficient funds to live on, and have no intention of seeking work. Self-employed people and entrepreneurs are welcome, provided they have enough capital to establish a new business or buy an existing one which provides employment for Canadian citizens or enriches Canadian cultural life.

Coastal climates are milder – the bitter cold winters in the middle of the country make first floor access to houses essential, because of the deep snow. Therefore Vancouver is very popular in the east and Toronto in the west.

An executive detached two-storey town house, on the out-skirts of Toronto, with four bedrooms, three baths, large family room with open fireplaces, and a two car heated garage attached, can be yours for £150,000. Most homes have a large basement, or recreational area, and all are exceptionally well-insulated and fitted with very effective heating/air-conditioning systems (they need to be, winter temperatures often fall to 20 degrees below freezing). A luxury apartment in the city centre, with two or three bedrooms, and under-floor heating, can be found for around the same price. Agents: OPB Ltd.

USA

Florida
The sunshine state, land of oranges, Disney World and the Everglades is by far the most popular with Britons seeking a holiday home in the USA. The range of property in Florida is enormous. Miami and Palm Beach are the traditional resorts on the east coast for holiday and retirement property, but these have tended to become overcrowded and expensive. Land for building is becoming scarce and this is pushing up prices. Further north, close to Orlando, the Palm Coast has more to offer and prices are reasonable. The west coast, with its seaboard on the Gulf of Mexico between St. Petersburg, Saratosa and Fort Myers, has also grown in popularity. Numerous new resorts have been created for permanent living — prices reflect the high demand.

Palm Beach is where the seriously rich people play. If you enjoy the high-life, £150,000 will buy you a 2,000 ft penthouse on the thirty-second floor, with three bedrooms, 'walk-in' closets (wardrobes), hot tub (bath), half bathroom (cloakroom) and commode (w.c.), overlooking the sea. The views will be stunning, facilities and services first class, but there may be restrictions on pets and children!

Then there are the Florida Keys, a captivating chain of 32 palm-fringed coral islets stretching like a necklace towards the Caribbean, and the Everglades national park with its incredible wildlife. Here £80,000 buys an opulent waterfront home, with five bedrooms, double garage, palm-fringed pool, sauna and whirlpool, private beach access and boat dock.

If you prefer the sugar white sand beaches and gentle waters of the Gulf of Mexico, then Naples, on Florida's south-west coast, is the place for you. More than 140 miles of waterways connect ultra-luxurious 'Condo's' and gracious houses, each more impressive than its neighbour. Wide boulevards, shaded by palms and banyans, bursting with bougainvillea, oliander, and hibiscus, and every garden a riot of exotic tropical blooms.

The climate is sub-tropical and the lifestyle infectious. It offers what Americans call the 'total leisure experience' – with tennis centres, polo fields, sailing, scuba-diving, windsurfing and golf courses wall-to-wall. The Philharmonic Performing Arts Centre and two 'live' theatres complete the cultural scene.

Luxurious 2,500 sq foot penthouse apartments overlooking the sea on the prestigious Gulf Shore Boulevard, command prices around £350,000. The cheapest two-bedroom bay-front condominium, surrounded by beautifully exotic gardens within the sound of the surf, costs around £69,000. Amenities within the complex typically include boat docks, exercise rooms, tennis courts, swimming pools and whirlpools, clubhouse with pool tables, large screen TV, and even office facilities with video ticker-tape display from the New York Stock Exchange.

At Pelican Bay, a three-bedroom house on the golf course, with cedar shingled roof and beautiful vaulted ceilings, kitchen with gourmet island and huge master suite, skylights and ceiling fans throughout, can be yours for £180,000 and the price includes swimming pool and screened lanai with sauna, whirlpool, grill and 'wet-bar'.

You do not have to pay a fortune for a home in Florida for buildings costs are not as high as they are in the UK. At Palm Coast, around 300 miles north of Miami, close to Orlando, one could buy a virtual palace for £120,000. At least five bedrooms, with sunken whirlpool tub on the terrace, and a six-seater Jaccuzi in the lounge, where you could live like a millionaire. Gardens are landscaped and irrigated, swimming pools are 'his' and 'hers' and the 250 sq. metre house on a 2,000 sq. metre plot can be built to individual specification.

A more modest two- or three-bedroomed house, with large family room, good utility kitchen, garage and plunge-pool in the 'yard' (garden), surrounded by neatly manicured lawns, can be built from £38,000, including the cost of the land. The surrounding development is low-key – ITP (America's fourth largest corporation) is only building on 40,000 of the 200,000 acre estate. Man and wildlife get along quite nicely here, with rivers full of fish (and the occasional alligator), natural woodlands, 80 miles of canals, four international golf courses, and 20 tennis courts.

Letting potential in Florida is good year-round – for a three bedroomed property in Palm Coast it is not unusual to gross around £250 per week. Rental rates in Naples and Palm Beach being proportionally higher.

Florida has excellent air links with all major US cities and the UK through Orlando and Miami international airports. Tampa and Daytona airports are also used frequently by visitors arriving from Britain. The flying time from London to Orlando or Miami is around eight hours, return airfares from £199 upwards. Agents: OPB Ltd.

California
House prices in California are around thirty per cent higher than those in Florida, but again this depends on the area. In the 'sought-after' areas in Beverley Hills, 'movie-star's' homes change hands for many millions of dollars. But one could still buy a traditional American-style ranch-house of generous proportions on the outskirts of Los Angeles for around £160,000.

When you buy a home in either place the price you pay will normally include fridge-freezer, 'stove' (not called a cooker in America) washing machine, microwave, dishwasher, even a food processor. Most homes are air-conditioned, and many come fully furnished. Prices are currently stable. Extreme caution should be taken if offered building plots outside approved development areas. The cost is unlikely to include power or water services, and connection could cost a small fortune.

A condominium, with a full maintenance programme, is an ideal choice for many non-residents. Buyers should take full note of any restrictive covenants, such as: No rentals, children or animals. It is also important to establish that the level of maintenance costs are controlled, and by whom.

In Florida, instead of paying rates on your property you pay a property tax of about 1 per cent of the value of your home, assessed every three years. Most communities levy a small charge for the maintenance of communal areas, but typically total taxes and charges are not likely to be more than £12 per week on a £50,000 property.

The roads that link the various centres in the USA are generally good. The Americans drive on the right; speed limits are lower than elsewhere in the world and are strictly enforced. Car-hire is relatively cheap and the cost of 'gas' (petrol) is less expensive than at home.

You can go and buy a home in America, if you have enough money, provided you have no intention of living there full time, whether for work or retirement. America does not readily permit immigration unless the applicants have close relatives already living there. A visitors' visa is acceptable for a visit of a few months each year. Alternatively, application for status of resident alien can be made. Under a recent change in US immigration law, British passport holders no longer require a visa if travelling to the USA from the UK on an approved airline, provided the visit is less than 90 days. It is essential that private health insurance is taken out, and this must be adequate for medical expenses are very high indeed.

Chapter Thirteen:
ADDING UP THE BILL

Nothing is straightforward when it comes to buying property and that goes for the costs as well. If you are thinking about buying abroad then it is vital to work out how much extra cash you'll need to fork out — both before and after you've received the key to the door.

Legal fees, transfer costs and taxes

As a rough rule of thumb you should expect to pay between 10% and 12% of the purchase price. This should cover taxes, transfer costs, two sets of legal fees and other liabilities. You should check with your lawyer at the outset all the charges you will have to meet over and above the purchase price. Practices vary from country to country. For example, in France it is quite common for the purchaser to foot the agent's bill rather than the seller as is the case here at home.

If you are planning to buy a property in Europe then you should be aware that the bulk of such transactions are completed before a public official known as a notary. It is their job to see that the rights of both buyer and seller are safeguarded. However a notary is not a substitute for a solicitor. Agreement in principle must be reached before going to the notary, so it is essential to have proper legal representation right from the word go.

Annual running costs

These vary tremendously. Much depends upon the area, type of property and quality of services provided. The maintenance charge on a two-bedroom flat in a modern serviced block in

Spain can range between £500 and £1,000 a year, depending on the quality of facilities being offered. Bills such as power, water and telephone will be on top. A villa is a more expensive option, security risks are higher and the garden will need to be tended.

Water and electricity supply
Always obtain a quote before reaching the contract stage. Connection charges on new properties can top £800. On homes which have already been linked to the main terminals you can expect to pay around £40 each for reconnecting the water and electricity in most European countries.

Beware the ruined stone cottage or derelict farmhouse tucked away off the beaten track. Unless your jungle instincts are well developed and you are happy to forego clean water and electricity you could face massive bills.

Insurance
Don't forget to take account of the cost of both buildings and contents insurance. Premiums are payable in advance. Comprehensive cover for buildings and contents insurance on an average two-bedroom holiday home in Europe will be in the region of £150.

Furnishing
Many developers offer villas and apartments fully furnished. If not, you should expect to pay out around £3,000 for a two-bedroom European flat.

Moving
How much this will set you back depends of course on whether you plan to take the contents of your British home with you, if for example you are retiring, or whether you plan to buy everything on site. The cost of moving around 70% of the contents of a two-bedroomed flat from England to Spain would be around £1,300 plus the cost of insurance.

Medical costs

Retired people, in particular, should consider the costs and quality of health care abroad. Often this is both more expensive and less efficient than the dear old National Health Service for all its faults. In some instances hefty medical bills have forced couples to sell up and return home, where to add insult to injury they're then faced a tax bill on the capital gain they had made on the overseas property.

Travelling

This will largely depend on the time of year you plan to use your home and the flexibility you require. Spur of the moment trips tend to cost extra unless there happens to be a surplus of seats just when you wish to take off.

How the costs add up

a) Couple retiring to Spain choosing a home priced at £40,000

Initial visit by couple	£350
Inspection flight	Free
Legal fees, tax, transfers	£4,000
Connection water and electricity	£80
One-year building and contents insurance	£150
Furniture, fittings	£3,000
Moving approx 50% belongings	£800
Total:	£8,380

b) Family of four buying a £20,000 cottage in France

Initial visit by family	£500
Legal fees, tax etc.	£2,000
Estate agent's fees*	£800
One-year insurance cover	£150
Connection water and electricity	£80

Repairs – kitchen and bath
Basic furnishing   £.

Total: £9,5.

British agents usually include these in the price quoted.

Covering a shortfall

Once you've totted up the likely bill, you may find you need to borrow some money to finance your purchase. Do be careful before taking on an additional financial burden. Try to view the transaction in the context of your overall position. Borrowing money is never cheap and you can't rely on the cost of your holiday home appreciating fast enough to cover the interest you will be shelling out.

The cost of obtaining finance for an overseas home can vary enormously. High street banks may offer you a personal loan over 10 years, at up to 7 per cent *over* bank base rate. Some foreign banks with branches in London might be prepared to lend you the money. The London branch of Banco de Bilbao will arrange mortgages of at least £5,000, and they will lend up to 60 per cent of the property's value. Repayments are fixed for ten years. Both the Banque Parisbas and the Banque Société Génerale can arrange mortgages on French properties and may lend up to 80 per cent of their value. Interest rates vary according to the currency you choose for the loan; 2 per cent *over* base rate in francs and sterling; and 3.5 per cent over base rate in Swiss francs.

Those wanting to buy a property in Spain should be able to get a loan from the Abbey National Building Society who offer these facilities from a subsidiary company in Gibraltar. The Abbey offers a complete buyers' package, including surveys and access to solicitors. Interest rates are slightly higher than at home.

You won't enjoy tax relief on a mortgage for an overseas home, so it might be cheaper to release some of the value wrapped up in your existing home in the UK. Several companies offer schemes specifically designed for British home-owners wishing to buy overseas property. Barclays Bank has extended its Home Mortgage Scheme for second or holiday homes abroad. Its scheme enables British residents to borrow up to 80 per cent of the value of their British property, which is then taken as security against the loan. Here's how it works. If the value of the existing home was £50,000, with a mortgage outstanding of £10,000, the resident could borrow up to £30,000 for pay for a holiday home. The maximum loan is £50,000 over five to fifteen years.

Mortgages of up to 80 per cent of the purchase price are available in Switzerland, repayable over a maximum of 25 years at relatively low interest rates, currently 8 per cent. No other commission is payable in respect of mortgage finance. There are two types of loan available, both guaranteed by the Swiss property. The first is an ordinary repayment mortgage, where interest payments are paid every six months, rather than monthly as at home.

The second type of mortgage is an overdraft facility. Interest payments are calculated on the outstanding balance. Although these will be higher in the earlier years, they will decline as the mortgage is paid off. The advantage of this sort of deal is that it offers a means of borrowing money cheaply. The borrower has the flexibility to pay off the loan immediately, without incurring any penalties, should exchange rates change in his favour.

For example, if you borrowed £100,000 and in 12 years time you had paid off half the loan, you would be able to borrow the full amount again, secured against the Swiss property. If in 12 years time interest rates in the UK are still high, and they are still relatively low in Switzerland (the Swiss franc is a stronger currency), then it might be extremely useful to be able to re-borrow the £50,000 repaid using the Swiss property as security.

Upkeep
Finally brace yourself for those unquantifiable costs which fall under the category of repairs and upkeep. As every homeowner knows only too well, boilers break down, loos leak and ceilings

crack. So allow some sort of financial cushion for repairs. You should budget for around 10%. Generally upkeep is usually cheaper in a warm climate than here at home. Villas and apartments normally need an annual clean.

Chapter Fourteen:
BUYING AND SELLING PROCEDURES

The golden rule to remember is never skimp on legal advice. A few hundred pounds spent hiring a solicitor at home and one in the country where you plan to buy can save you literally thousands of pounds which you could lose if the transaction turns sour.

Buying property is always fraught with hazards – and these are multiplied when you are dealing with a foreign legal system and negotiations are conducted in a tongue you do not understand.

A full list of solicitors who specialise in handling property transactions abroad is in Section D. There is also a list of foreign banks with branches in the UK. They can prove a useful source of advice on any currency restrictions or formalities about the best way to transfer money.

Buyers' Checklist
Before you get down to the nitty-gritty of the transaction check:

★The person offering the property does in fact own it. Watch out for joint ownerships.

★Foreigners are permitted to buy property. Some countries, such as Turkey, restrict foreign ownership in certain areas.

★There are no outstanding mortgages. When you buy property in countries such as Spain, you also take over debts secured

90

on the property. All outstanding utilities bills should be settled by the vendor.

★All the necessary planning approval has been granted.

★Any rules on transferring money into the country and then taking it out again.

★The contract discloses the true price paid for the house. You might save on taxes and registration dues in the short-term by underdeclaring, but you'll have a large capital gain on paper when you sell up.

★The builder undertakes to connect mains services to the house and to make up roads.

★If necessary, rules of residence.

★Any restrictions on letting.

Andorra
Possibly the cheapest place in the world to buy a home. There is no stamp duty and no property tax. You will pay a small fee of about ½% of the purchase price to the notary and a token sum to the local estate agent.

Again, as elsewhere on the Continent, the notary acts as middle man. Two documents are involved, an 'escriptura publica' simply stating the sale has been transacted and an 'escriptura privado' stating the financial and legal details. No capital gains tax here and no restrictions on transferring your money around the world.

Australia
Legal and conveyancing charges vary from state to state, but buying costs should not amount to more than 10 per cent of the purchase price. There is no capital gains to pay when you sell your Australian home.

Bahamas
Bahamian law is based on the British, and procedures for property purchase are much the same.

Barbados

There are no restrictions on British people buying property in Barbados. However, purchase tax of around 17 per cent is incurred, plus any legal fees. There is no capital gains tax to pay when you sell your home in Barbados.

British Virgin Islands

Property transfer in the British Virgin Islands is relatively straightforward. Buyers pay a 5 per cent stamp duty, based on the cost of the property and a further 1 per cent should be allowed for legal fees. There is no capital gains tax to pay when you sell your British Virgin Islands home.

Canada

Buying a property in Canada takes no time at all. Once the buyer has signed an intention to buy, paying a deposit of 10–12 per cent, he then has 10 days to check out the property, carry out searches and surveys etc. After 10 days he will forfeit his deposit if he decides not to go ahead with the property. No gazumping here – the seller must let the buyer have the first option.

Mortgages are arranged through banks, trust or insurance companies and credit unions – the maximum loan is 75 per cent of purchase price. Interest rates are currently around 11–12 per cent. There are currently no restrictions on foreigners buying property. However, most provinces levy a tax of around 20 per cent on the purchase price of property by non residents.

Cayman Islands

Property purchase in the Cayman Islands is relatively uncomplicated. There are no taxes to pay, but stamp duty of 7½ per cent of the purchase price is paid by the purchaser.

Cyprus

The legal system is based on English law, and the system of property transfer and registration is relatively simple. However, securing proper title to a newly-built property can take rather a long time. Before the Land Registry will issue a title on a new home, the developer is obliged to complete everything from roads to leisure facilities. If you are planning to buy a new home then lodge a copy of the developer's contract with the Registry as quickly as possible.

That aside, pick a local solicitor with a good reputation. A register of English speaking lawyers can be found in local courts; most speak English anyway. Remember, when you come to sell that although there is no capital gains tax you can only take your money out of the country very slowly – at the rate of around £6,000 a year.

France

One snag is that in France, all fees, about 15 per cent of the purchase price, including 45 per cent for the estate agent, must be paid by the purchaser (Most British agents selling French property include their fees in the quoted price, but do check).

The first step after choosing your property is to draw up a preliminary contract which describes the property and the price. This is then duly signed by both parties in front of the local official known as the notaire (notary).

At this stage you will have to pay a deposit, usually about 10 per cent which will only be refunded if you cannot proceed for financial reasons. Upon receipt of the necessary funds in French francs, the notaire will draw up the 'acte de vente' – the deed of sale – for you to sign. The property then belongs to you. Make sure you obtain a certified copy of the sale deed and register it with the appropriate land registry.

Legal fees are around 2½ per cent. Then there is a 5 per cent conveyancing tax and ½ per cent property tax based on the value of your purchase. Make sure VAT was included in the original price, otherwise you could be in for a nasty shock. VAT on new homes can rise to 17½ per cent and there may be a 3½ per cent registration fee if it is new property. On resales the VAT is usually around 7 per cent to 8 per cent. When you sell your home, you will be asked to leave a deposit covering your tax bill with the local notary.

If you sell your French home within two years of purchase

you must pay 33.6 per cent of the profit in capital gains tax. Keep any receipts for restoration work as these can be set against your final tax bill. The longer you hold on to the property the less tax you pay. A sale is only free of French taxes after 22 years of ownership.

Gibraltar
The legal system is based on English law, and so property transfer and registration procedures hardly differ. There are plenty of British solicitors based in Gibraltar.

Italy
The initial contract is in the form of a legal promise to proceed and involves financial penalties for either party if they decide against going ahead. Again, the buyer forfeits the deposit and the seller has to pay double the sum deposited.

The lynchpin in the transaction is once again the notary. This time the notary will check out the legal background to the property and make sure it can be sold by the person involved. The notary will also require a document to show that you have brought the money to pay for the property into the country through legally acceptable channels.

From here on in things can get a bit hairy. Make sure you have adequate local legal and tax advice. You may find yourself involved in intense bargaining over the stated purchase price and without a good local solicitor could end up in deep water.

Buying in Italy is very expensive and you should ask your solicitor to calculate the extra taxes involved at the outset. Stamp duty, paid by the purchaser, ranges from 10 to 17 per cent. All in all you should allow about 15 per cent of the purchase price to cover legal fees, transfer costs and tax.

Life is never straight forward here. Provided the original payment methods met the required regulations you can take your money out of the country again. Capital gains tax on the profits range from 5 per cent to 30 per cent depending on length of ownership.

Malta

Compared to Italy, Maltese procedures are reasonably plain sailing. A preliminary contract is signed, the local notary performs the search and three months later you should receive the final deed of sale. You will have to provide evidence of where the money to buy the property came from, and if you are planning to retire obtain a residence permit. The costs work out at around 5.5 per cent of the purchase price plus legal fees. So together you should end up paying around 10 per cent.

One sticking problem here is the Maltese government requirement that, if you sell, you first offer the property to local residents at what is deemed to be a reasonable price. Problems can arise if you disagree with the government approved price. Only if this is not taken up can you try for a possibly higher price from another foreigner. However there is no local capital gains tax.

Portugal

The first legal act is to draw up a provisional contract of sale, known as the 'contrato de promessa de compra a venda'. This states the buying and selling conditions plus an official promise by both parties to go ahead with the transaction. If either parties decided to pull out there are financial penalties. You the buyer will forfeit your deposit and the seller must pay the would-be buyer twice the deposit.

Completion takes place before a state notary, who will keep the original contract of sale and register the transfer of property. You will receive an official copy of the title deeds in your name and must then register your ownership with the Land Registry. It is important to receive prior permission from the Banco de Portugal which issues a licence enabling you to bring in the necessary money for the purchase – and to take it out again should you decide to sell.

You will pay a 10 per cent transfer tax, SISA, on a completed building costing over 10 million Escudos (around £50,000), a 1 per cent fee to the notary and local legal fees of around 2 per cent. However the SISA tax is exempt for first time buyers paying under £50,000. Here, capital gains tax is deducted from your profits. You are then free to transfer the proceeds to the country of your choice.

Spain

There are two sorts of local lawyers who can be involved in conveyancing in Spain. The powers of the notario are strictly limited. He acts as a public official and certifies that the contract is prepared, signed and authenticated in accordance with the law. He is not concerned with the actual contract and he won't carry out any searches for you – make sure this is done by your lawyer.

Your solicitor should obtain a copy of the seller's escritura or title deed, showing the address of the property and the registration number. He can then order an up-to-date extract – a nota simple – which will give details of the ownership of the property and of any mortgages on it. He should get a further nota simple just before you sign the escritura in your favour, to make sure no mortgages have been taken out in the interim.

Your solicitor should draw up a private contract of purchase giving all the vital details including legal description, price, payment, completion and possession dates. This is then duly signed by both parties in front of the local official known as the public notary.

Once the contract has been signed, you will be asked for a deposit. The acceptable figure for this is 10 per cent. Don't be talked into anything higher. Completion is usually within thirty to sixty days.

On completion, when the full price has been paid, you will be given a deed of conveyance – known as an 'escritura'. This is then assessed for taxes and sent to the Property Registry, so details of the new owner can be recorded.

There is a 6 per cent tax calculated on the purchase price. Land for development is taxed at 12 per cent. These taxes are the Spanish version of value added tax and referred to as IVA. Once you have added in legal fees and transfer costs your final bill is likely to be 10 per cent of the purchase price.

Don't make the final payment until you have:
★ A certificate of finished work from the architect.

* A habitation certificate issued by the local authority.
* A certificate of electrical installation to enable you to be connected to the mains supply.
* A confirmation that the water supply has been connected.

Just as in France, you can repatriate your profits less local capital gains tax provided pesetas were used originally. There is no tax free break for those owning a property for any period of time.

Switzerland

Before you can buy Swiss property you must obtain permission from the local canton and from the central government in Berne. A notary acts for both parties and registers the change of ownership at the Land Registry. The first step is to sign a 'Promesse de Vente' (a contract to purchase) and pay a 10 per cent deposit. The notary then requests permission from the local canton and from the central government in Berne for the sale to be approved.

A sale to the foreigner will generally only be refused if he or she already owns a Swiss property. A contract is always conditional on authorisation being granted and the process takes about eight weeks. The buyer must agree any mortgage arrangements before signing the Definitive Act which is the final transfer.

Notary's fees and land registry fees amount to 1.7 per cent of the purchase price. The buyer will also pay a one off tax of 3.3 per cent of the property value. There is no VAT in Switzerland so the total buying costs should not exceed 5.5 per cent, including legal fees.

Rules on resale are strict. You must not sell your Swiss home for at least five years, and then only to a Swiss. After 10 years you may be allowed to sell to a non-Swiss resident. Regulations vary from one canton to another, check with the local notary.

Death duties are payable in Switzerland, but these are much lower than at home, usually between 2 per cent and 7 per cent of the value of the property.

You must use your Swiss home for at least three weeks a year, and you may let it for a maximum of 11 months. You will not be taxed in Switzerland upon any letting income, although if you are resident in the UK the British tax-man will want his share. Most people have their rental income paid into a numbered Swiss bank account and have standing orders for maintenance payments and other expenses paid out of that account.

Turkey

Special care should be taken when entering any leasehold arrangement, particularly if it's with an individual, rather than a bank or large licenced company. The ownership of a lease must be registered at the local land registry at the time of purchase, and re-registered every 10 years to remain valid.

For leaseholds the land registry charge is only 0.3 per cent. Buying costs also include stamp duty and notary fees, adding a further 1.5 per cent. If you are buying a freehold you should allow about 12 per cent on top of the purchase price to cover taxes, transfer costs and other liabilities. Funds for the purchase must be transferred direct from your bank at home.

There should be no problem repatriating your money when you sell, provided the funds for the original purchase were transferred through proper banking channels. Capital gains tax will not apply unless the Turkish property has been owned for less than a year.

USA

Property purchase in the USA is simple, inexpensive and safe. The sale contract should be very comprehensive and outline all costs involved. A copy of any restrictive convenants should also be enclosed as they may prohibit sub-letting, or in the case of some condominiums, no children or pets may be allowed.

To reserve a property, a deposit of around 10 per cent will be required upon signing the contract, followed by either payment in full on completion, or stage payments as outlined in the contract. An attorney (lawyer) will charge around £300 for handling the entire transaction; the only other legal cost being £10 for the registration of the deed.

Interest rates on home loans are lower than in the UK,

currently around 7–9 per cent, over 15 to 30 years. An arrangement fee of 3–5 per cent of the sum borrowed is levied by the broker, but this will cover all state and federal taxes. Most mortgage companies will require buildings insurance costing around £200 on a £50,000 property. Sales of American property involve a 20 per cent capital gains tax on any profit.

Tax points

Provided you stuck to the rules about bringing in currency to the country of your choice, you should have few problems when you come to sell. You will end up with a tax bill – both here at home and usually in the country where your property was located. Keep a note of taxes you pay abroad as these can usually be offset against your tax bill at home. Don't forget that although there is no capital gains tax on profits from sale of your main home in the UK, you will have to pay tax on any gains over and above your annual allowance made from your overseas home.

Letting

Don't forget, you will have to declare any income you earn from letting to the UK tax authorities if you are still resident in Britain. You will pay income tax on these earnings. For higher rate taxpayers this may remove the attractions involved in letting your property.

Offshore solution

Many people investing overseas decide to create an offshore company to help reduce some of the potential pitfalls. Readers are advised to seek professional advice on this matter. Those considering buying a property in Spain would do well to consider this option as local inheritance laws can generate a multitude of problems which you may be able to minimise by opting to set up an offshore company.

Chapter Fifteen:
TIMESHARING

Ten years ago the word timesharing would not have meant much to the average Englishman. Even now after a mixed press the concept of timesharing is only hazily understood.

In simple terms, timesharing means buying the right to use a specific property for a designated number of weeks, at a chosen time of year, for a specified number of years. It can also mean the purchase of an actual share in the freehold of a property. The price will be determined by the length of time purchased, and the chosen season. If you want a change of scene or season, there are timeshare-swop organisations that will help you.

The concept of timesharing isn't new. The idea of buying a furnished home – be it a flat, house, villa or cottage – for a chosen number of weeks every year, was first introduced at a ski resort in the French Alps, in 1967. It was then adopted by the American developers, when massive US interest rates in the 1970s led the government to forbid banks making loans on second homes. Timesharing was the obvious solution; it helped to fill empty apartment blocks, and soon became popular with American buyers.

In 1987 the leading timeshare operators set up an association in an attempt to spruce up the industry's image and establish minimum levels of standards. But unfortunately timeshare is still an area which appeals to the cowboys. What after all could be nicer than selling a slice of the same property over and over again – or even more profitable, a slice of property not yet built.

The lack of a legally enforcible 'cooling off' or cancellation period is a major source of complaint. Deposits are often non-returnable and customers who sign credit agreements have no legal right to their money back if they have a change of heart later on. Other problems include pressure to sign on the spot, and not being allowed to show sales documents to a solicitor. Misleading information about 'cooling-off' periods, given to customers as an inducement to sign, has led to buyers losing all, or at least part of their deposit, if they decide not to go ahead with a timeshare purchase.

There have been cases of out and out fraud, where the property being sold is just a hole in the ground. Some buyers have paid thousands of pounds up-front for timeshare apartments not yet built, sometimes without planning permission. There have also been problems with annual maintenance. Many purchasers complain about poorly maintained timeshare properties and annual charges which rise uncontrollably; in some cases doubling in less than a year. Owners are also reporting difficulties with the resale of timeshares — resale is expensive, often slow and virtually impossible if the developer still has units to sell.

When it comes to buying timeshare, time is on your side, so take plenty of it to consider the offer. You may find the following checklist useful:

Checklist

★Don't sign anything or pay any money at the first meeting with the salesman and ignore all pressure to sign up on the spot for a discount, or any other inducement you are offered.

★Demand full details in writing of what is being offered, including the price, and don't deal with people who refuse to let you take away the relevant documents.

★Ask a solicitor to have a look at the contract or any other documents before committing yourself to anything.

★It is vital to find out all the details about maintenance charges and what they cover. They can be as much as £200 a week and are likely to rise after you have bought. Check how the increases are to be decided and by whom. Is there an owners' association to represent your interests, and can it dismiss the management company if it falls down on the job?

★Try to ascertain what your position would be if the developer went bankrupt. Would your timeshare rights be protected?

★Be especially careful if you are approached on holiday. If you do decide to visit a timeshare resort, leave your chequebook and credit cards at the hotel – and don't tell the salesman they are there, or he may offer you a lift back to collect them.

★Make sure you are dealing with a reputable company. Members of the Timeshare Developers Association have a code of conduct, which includes a minimum five-day cooling off period. However, the Office of Fair Trading which is currently investigating timeshare, has received a number of complaints about TDA members who do not honour their code of conduct. Some impose penalties for cancellation and you might only get part of your deposit back if you decide not to go ahead with a purchase.

Barratt Multi-Ownership, the holiday-timeshare division of British housebuilders, who own three resorts on Spain's Costa del Sol, and seven in Britain, is one of the better companies. They offer a guaranteed seven-day cooling-off period, with no financial penalties – the same does not hold true for some other notable British companies who own timeshare resorts.

★If you want to swop your timeshares it will need to be affiliated to one of the international timeshare exchange companies – Interval International or RCI. But, you will also have to pay at least £45 per week swoped.

Alternatives
To avoid the pitfalls involved in timesharing, alternatives have been formulated which retain the basic concept. The largest is the Swiss-based Hapimag Property Club, which is a kind of vacationers' co-operative. This system has, in fact, been operating for over twenty-two years, before conventional timeshare

began, and its members now own more than forty resorts throughout Europe.

The difference between this scheme and ordinary timeshare is that buyers do not purchase a share in any particular property. Instead they buy shares in the company itself at around £1,500 each. This allows them to choose from resorts in Spain, Greece, Italy, France, Austria, Germany and Switzerland and Finland, for a fixed period every year, usually around two weeks. Shareholders also get access to other resorts worldwide, through an arrangement with RCI.

For a basic share the buyer gets twelve holiday points on a credit system. A total of twenty-four points (£4,000) entitles a family of four to a one to three week holiday in high season, depending on the resort, and up to six weeks in low season. Each resort and property is allocated a specific number of points. For twenty-four points, four people could have three summer weeks in Tenerife, or a week's peak-season skiing in Switzerland. Another £50 would be payable per holiday week, per year, for service charges.

A computerised booking system is flexible enough to cope with as little as forty-eight hours notice, before departure. The computer also makes sure that members who cannot get their first holiday-choice one year, get priority the next.

Hapimag shares are owned in perpetuity, and protected by Swiss law, shares may also be inherited. Secondly, if you change your mind, you can sell your shares to Hapimag after four years, at current market price, currently 2,550 less 18 per cent management charges. Agents: Comser International, Orantecq House, Fairview Road, Timperley, WA15 7AR Tel 061 904 9750.

How to complain

Complaints about timeshare should be made in writing to the Office of Fair Trading in London. Alternatively, contact the nearest Citizens Advice Bureau and ask for the address of your local Trading Standards Officer.

Chapter Sixteen:
AGENTS AND DEVELOPERS

Association of British Overseas Property Agents
    and Consultants,
Orient House,
42–45 New Broad Street,
London
EC2.

Federation of Overseas Property Developers, Agents
    and Consultants,
Imperial House,
15–19 Kingsway,
London
WC2B 6UU.
Tel: 071-836 1840

National Association of Estate Agents,
Arbon House,
21 Jury Street,
Warwick
CV34 4EH.
Tel: 0926-4968000

CISA Andorran Properties Ltd.,
12 Kings College Road,
Ruislip,
Middlesex
HA4 8BH.
Tel: 0895-621617

CISA Construccio Immobiliaria S.A.,
Ed. La Cabanota,
La Massana,
Principality of Andorra.
Tel: 35228/35055

Gestandor UK Ltd.,
Office 13, 5th Floor,
25 Victoria Street,
London
SW1.
Tel: 071-222 3138

Invico Ltd.,
Broomholm,
Langholm,
Dumfriesshire.
Tel: 0541-80818

Sunshine Associates,
Bridge House,
Winters Bridge,
Thames Ditton,
Surrey.
Tel: 081-398 4746

Villas Abroad (Properties) Ltd.,
55 York Street,
Twickenham,
Middlesex
TW1 3LL.
Tel: 081-891 5444

AUSTRALIA

SPECIALISED AREA

O.P.B. Ltd.,
1 Woodlands,
Manor Road,
Penn,
Buckinghamshire
HP10 8SD.

CANADA

SPECIALISED AREA

O.P.B. Ltd.,
1 Woodlands,
Manor Road,
Penn,
Buckinghamshire
HP10 8SD.

CARIBBEAN

SPECIALISED AREA

Smiths Gore International (Chartered Surveyors)
Fielden House,
Little College Street,
Westminster,
London SW1 3SH.
Tel: 071-222 4054

CYPRUS

SPECIALISED AREA

Leptos UK Ltd.,
451 West Green Road,
London
N15.
Tel: 081-881 3356

Spanish Property Investments,
Astra House,
19 The Mall,
Bromley,
Kent.
Tel: 081-460 9910

VillaMed Properties (Cyprus & Greece),   Limassol and Paphos.
5 Sleaford Road,
Branston,
Lincoln
LN4 1LL.
Tel: 0522-793065

Whiteway Properties,
Suite 2,
12 High Street,
Knaresborough,
North Yorkshire.
Tel: 0423-865892/867047 and 071-834 1005

FRANCE   SPECIALISED AREA

David Scott International,   Ski apartments.
Deerhurst House,
Epping Road,
Roydon,
Harlow,
Essex.
Tel: 027979-2162

Frank Rutherford French Property Consultants,
7 Chelsea Manor Street,
London SW3.
Tel: 071-351 4454

French and Associates
Robertsbridge House
Robertsbridge,
Sussex.
Tel: 0580 880699

John Alexander,
174 Edmund Street,
Birmingham
B3 2HD.
Tel: 021-236 0874

Kenneth Ward & Co.,
Exchange House,
77 Laleham Road,
Staines,
Middlesex.
Tel: 0990-22275

Maurice Lazarus,   South of France: St Tropez,
Florida Centre,   Provence, French Alps.
4 Gardnor Road,
Hampstead,
London
NW3 1HA.
Tel: 071-409 0571

Mills & Co.,   La Plagne, French Alps.
Ryall Mead,
Holly Green,
Upton-Upon-Severn,
Worcester.
Tel: 06846-3921

Montpelier International,   South of France.
17 Montpelier Street,
London
SW7.
Tel: 071-589 3400

Villas Abroad (Properties) Ltd.,   Alps, Côte d'Azur,
55 York Street,   S.W. and Atlantic coasts.
Twickenham,
Middlesex
TW1 3LL.
Tel: 081-891 5444

Ward Turner,
862 Bristol Road,
Selly Oak,
Birmingham
B29 6HW
Tel: 021-472 6141

Woodham Estates,   Thollon Les Menusis, Haute Savoie.
3 Guildford Road,
Woking,
Surrey.
Tel: 04862-60229/69754

GIBRALTAR   SPECIALISED AREA

P.M.S.,
Wesley House,
Main Street,
Gibraltar.
Tel: 010-350 71428

The Property Shop,
International House,
Bell Lane,
Gibraltar.
Tel: 010-350 77876/76348

Trafalgar Business and Property Services,
104/6 Irish Town,
Gibraltar.
Tel: 010-350 70903

ITALY

Euro-Property Advisers,
27a New Street,
Salisbury
SP1 2PH.
Tel: 0722-330847

Italian Country Homes,
Kelly House,
Warwick Road,
Tunbridge Wells,
TN1 1YL
Tel: 0892-515611

Italian Properties,
The Old Telephone Exchange,
Pershore Road,
Eckington,
Tel: 0386 750133

MALTA

Frank Salt Real Estate,
2 Pacevile Avenue,
St Julians,
Malta.
Tel: Malta 337373 or 335175

PORTUGAL

Algarve Homes Ltd.,
Anzec House,
Stour St.,
Canterbury,
Kent
CT1 2NR.
Tel: 0227-69292

SPECIALISED AREA

Italy and Sardinia.

Tuscany, Umbria and Sardinia.

SPECIALISED AREA

SPECIALISED AREA

Beach Villas,   Algarve.
55 Sidney Street,
Cambridge,
CB2 3HX.
Tel: 0223-350777

Bovis Lakeside Village,
62 Brompton Road,
London
SW3.
Tel: 071-225 0411

Corinthian International,
168 Sloane Street,
London
SW1X 9LF.
Tel: 071-235 8981

David Scott International,   Algarve.
Deerhurst House,
Epping Road,
Roydon,
Harlow,
Essex.
Tel: 027979-2162

Euro-Property Advisers,   Algarve.
27a New Street,
Salisbury
SP1 2PH.
Tel: 0722-330847

Kenneth Ward & Co.,
Exchange House,
77 Laleham Road,
Staines,
Middlesex.
Tel: 0990-22275

Longcroft Properties Ltd.,
155 Whiteladies Road,
Bristol
BS8 2RG.
Tel: 0272-743925 (24 hours)

Savills Estate Agents,
132–135 Sloane Street,
London
SW1X 9AX.
Tel: 071-730 0822

SPAIN, MAJORCA, MINORCA & IBIZA   SPECIALISED AREA

Beach Villas,   Costa Brava, Costa Blanca,
55 Sidney Street,   Costa del Sol, Majorca, Minorca.
Cambridge
CB2 3HX.
Tel: 0223-350777

Bendinat/Anchorage Waterfront Village   Majorca.
London Office,
Collier House,
163–9 Brompton Road,
London
SW3 1HW.
Tel: 071–589 4567

Bovis Abroad,   Costa del Sol, Costa Blanca.
62 Brompton Road,
London
SW3.
Tel: 071-225 0411

The Chesham Group of Companies,   Spain.
9 London Road,
Newbury,
Berkshire
RG13 1JL.
Tel: 0635-49900

Coope and Co. (Properties) Ltd.,
66/67 High Street,
Lymington,
Hampshire.
Tel: 0590-77971

Crystal Properties,   Costa Blanca, Costa Brava.
Thornden House,
17 Joy Lane,
Whitstable,
Kent
CT5 4LS.

David Scott International,   Costa del Sol.
Deerhurst House,
Epping Road,
Roydon,
Harlow,
Essex.
Tel: 027979-2162

T. K. Espana (UK) Ltd.,   Costa del Sol.
37/41 Bedford Row,
London
WC1R 4JH.
Tel: 071-831 7607

Euro-Properties Advisers   Costa del Sol, Marbella,
27a New Street,   Sotogrande Estate.
Salisbury SP1 2PH
Tel: 0722 330847

Fincasol,   Costa del Sol.
4 Bridge Street,
Salisbury,
Wiltshire.
Tel: 0722-26444

Gestandor UK Ltd.,
Office 13, 5th Floor,
25 Victoria Street,
London
SW1.
Tel: 071-222 3183

Costa Brava, Costa Dorada.

Goodwin Duffy Estates,
194/196 Waterloo Street,
Burton-on-Trent,
Staffordshire
DE14 2NQ.
Tel: 0283-48191/2 and 38835

Hannah and Company,
29 Townhead Street,
Strathaven,
Strathclyde,
ML10 6AB.
Tel: 0357-20683/20163

Costa del Sol.

Headland Overseas,
67 Wellingborough Road,
Rushden,
Northamptonshire.
Tel: 0926-42441

East Coast.

Hidalgo International Ltd.,
45 Leas Road,
Warlingham,
Surrey.
CR3 9LP.
Tel: 08832-6019

Torre del Mar, Nerja.

Holkers Estate Agents,
The Avenue,
Leigh,
Lancashire.
Tel: 0942-671129/605986

Torre del Mar, Costa del Sol.

Iberian Property Associates,   Costa del Sol.
65a Kingsland Road,
Worthing,
West Sussex
BN14 9ED.
Tel: 0903-36254

Interspain Services UK Ltd.,   Southern Spain.
Suite 2,
66–72 High Street,
Rayleigh,
Essex.
Tel: 0268-775165

I.P.I.,   Northern Spain, Costa Brava,
34 Ship Street,   Costa Blanca, Minorca, Majorca and
Brighton,   Canary Islands.
Sussex.
Tel: 0273-724369

John Alexander,
174 Edmund Street,
Birmingham
B3 2HD.
Tel: 021-236 0874

John Compass Ltd.,
142 Rose Street,
Edinburgh,
Scotland.
Tel: 031-225 5166

Joule Estates,
450 Didsbury Road,
Heaton Mersey,
Stockport,
Greater Manchester
SK4 3BS.
Tel: 061-432 7070

Juan Porsellanes SA,   Spain.
50 Wellington Road,
Enfield,
Middlesex.
Tel: 081-363 8824

Kenneth Ward & Co.,   Spain, Majorca, Minorca and Ibiza.
Exchange House,
77 Laleham Road,
Staines,
Middlesex.
Tel: 0990-22275

La Nao/Bradley & Vaughan Overseas Ltd.   Javea, Denia
34–36 The Broadway,   and Moraira.
Haywards Heath,
RH16 3A1.
Tel: 0444-412551

Leslie Marsh & Co.,   Majorca.
71 Masbro Road,
London
W14.
Tel: 071-603 5181

Mintegui Immobilliearia,   Majorca.
Obispo Campina 12–12B,
Palma de Majorca,
Spain.
Tel: Parma 213944

Miraflores (UK) Ltd.,   Costa del Sol
116 College Road,
Harrow,
Middlesex
HA1 1BZ.
Tel: 081-863 0811

116

Overseas Residential Properties Ltd.,   Southern Spain.
5 Broadway Court,
Buckinghamshire
HP5 1DB.
Tel: 0494-791779

Puerto Sotogrande   Costa del Sol.
3 Shepherds Market,
London
W1Y 7HS
Tel: 071-495 3630

The Reysea Group,   Costa Blanca, Costa Calida.
14a Chine Avenue,
Bitterne,
Southampton
SO2 7JF.
Tel: 0703-443730

Savills Estate Agents,   Costa del Sol
132–5 Sloane Street,
London
SW1X 9AX.
Tel: 071-730 0822

Scotchbrooks International,   Costa del Sol, Costa Blanca.
29 Friar Street,
Reading,
RD1 1DP.
Tel: 0734-585181

Spanish Property Investments,   Costa del Sol, Costa Blanca.
Astra House,
19 The Mall,
Bromley,
Kent.
Tel: 081-460 9910

Stanton Property & Dev. Ltd.,   Spain.
Eagle House,
Cranleigh Close,
South Croydon,
Surrey.
Tel: 081-651 2855

Sturgis International,   Marbella.
139 Park Lane,
London
W1.
Tel: 071-493 1693

Sun Ibiza Ltd.,   Ibiza.
42 Aylesbury Road,
Bromley,
Kent
BR2 OQR.
Tel: 081-290 0094

Sunrise Overseas Properties,   Torreveja, Costa Blanca.
Sackville Place,
44/8 Magdalen Street,
Norwich.
Tel: 0603-615692

Sunshine Associates,
Bridge House,
Winters Bridge,
Thames Ditton,
Surrey.
Tel: 081-398 4746

Spanish Property Investments,
Astra House,
19 The Mall,
Bromley,
Kent.
Tel: 081-460 9910

Vernon Smith European,   Majorca.
38 Bell Street,
Reigate,
Surrey.
Tel: 07372-46868

Villa Antonita,
La Isleta,
Campello,
Alicante,
Spain.
Tel: 965-632276

Ward Turner,   Costa del Sol, Costa Blanca,
862 Bristol Road,   Majorca, Minorca.
Selly Oak,
Birmingham,
B29 6HW.
Tel: 021-472 6141

Whiteway Properties,
Suite 2,
12 High Street,
Knaresborough,
North Yorkshire.
Tel: 0423-865892/867047 and 071-834 1005

TENERIFE AND LANZAROTE

Aer Lingus Espana,   Sansofe, Tenerife.
Sansofe,
Puerto Santiago,
Santiago del Teide,
Tenerife,
Spain.

Castillo Sur,   S. Tenerife
Avenida Suecia 18,
Los Cristianos 38650,
S. Tenerife.
Tel: 01034-22792319

Chilcott White and Company Ltd.,
125 South End,
Croydon,
Surrey
CR9 1AR.
Tel: 081-688 4151

Cooper and Co., (Properties),
66/67 High Street,
Lymington,
Hampshire.
Tel: 0590-77971

Goodwin Duffy Estates,
194/196 Waterloo Street,
Burton-on-Trent,
Staffordshire.
Tel: 0283-48191/2

I.P.I.,   Tenerife.
34 Ship Street,
Brighton,
Sussex.
Tel: 0273-724369

John Alexander,
174 Edmund Street,
Birmingham
B3 2HD.
Tel: 021-236 0874

Kenneth Ward & Co.,
Exchange House,
77 Laleham Road,
Staines,
Middlesex.
Tel: 0990-22275

Sunshine Associates,
Bridge House,
Winters Bridge,
Thames Ditton,
Surrey.
Tel: 071-398 4746

SWITZERLAND

Osbornes,
93 Parkway,
London
NW1 7PP.
Tel: 071-485 8811

IPI Ltd.,
34 Ship Street,
Brighton,
Sussex.
Tel: 0273-724369

TURKEY

Tavnerstar Ltd.,
Dominic House,
171–177 London Road,
Kingston-upon-Thames,
Surrey.
Tel: 081-549 9236

SPECIALISED AREA

Bodrum.

UNITED STATES OF AMERICA

O.P.B. Ltd.,
1 Woodlands,
Manor Road,
Penn,
Buckinghamshire
HP10 8SD.

SPECIALISED AREA

Florida.

OTHER ADDRESSES

British Association of Removers,
277 Grays Inn Road,
London
WC1X 8SY.
Tel: 071-837 3088

Law Society,
113 Chancery Lane,
London
WC2A 1PL.
Tel: 071-242 1222

Royal Institution of Chartered Surveyors,
12 George Street,
London
SW1.
Tel: 071-222 7000

Training For Your Next Career
Margaret Korving

More and more people are choosing to change careers in mid-stream or perhaps, are forced to make a change due to redundancy. In this timely guide Margaret Korving shows you how to revolutionise your working life. She explains simply and clearly the choices open to you, the range of courses, variety of teaching methods and the cost of retraining.

It includes:
- Combining work with study
- On the job training and government schemes
- Studying from home
- Getting a degree
- Technician, craft, commercial professional courses

Your Green Career
Helen D'Arcy and Gillian Sharp

Can you stay green and still have a financially rewarding
job? The authors of this book show you how. It is packed
with practical advice on training, pay and job opportunities.
It includes interviews with people working in ''green'' jobs
across the country and shows you how to turn your talents
into a green career.

It includes:
- Healthy Alternatives
- Food For Thought
- Tilling The Soil
- All Creatures Great and Small
- The Great Outdoors
- National Heritage
- New Scientist
- Quality Control
- Building The Future

Fresh Start
Your Guide To Changing Careers By Men and Women Who Have Done It.
Dennis Barker

The symptoms are all too familiar. Lethargy, depression, inability to concentrate or cope with the daily grind at work. But, don't despair. It is possible to revitalise your life, reassess your priorities and rediscover that elusive job satisfaction. Dennis Barker, author and journalist, has talked to many people who have revolutionised their lives by the simple step of changing their careers. In this book they share their experiences and give positive guidance to others who may be contemplating a fresh start of their own.

It includes:
- Warning Signs
- Family Pressures Trap
- Paths to Giving
- Back to School
- Financial Step-down
- Resisting Ill Luck

All titles available at bookshops. If you have any problem getting the book you require, please contact the publishers Rosters Ltd at 23 Welbeck St, London W1M 7PG. Tel: 071-935 4550.